MUGABE

Teacher, Revolutionary, Tyrant

ANDREW NORMAN

Front cover image: Mugabe addresses the crowd as part of his official birthday celebrations, 26 February, 2005, Marondera. He was 81 on 21 February that year. The scarf (tied on by his wife Grace) is the symbol of the 21st February youth movement. Known by the brutalised Zimbabwean populace simply as 'the youth', its members are used to intimidate and punish all those who oppose the leader. The red in the Zimbabwean flag represents blood – the blood of sacrifice in the struggle against the colonial regime and apartheid. Here, it represents more accurately the crimes of a man steeped in his own nation's blood. © Howard Burditt/Reuters/Corbis

First published 2008

The History Press Ltd
The Mill, Brimscombe Port
Stroud, Gloucestershire, GL5 2QG
www.thehistorypress.co.uk

British Library Cataloguing in Publication Data.
A catalogue record for this book is available from the British Library.

ISBN 978 1 86627 491 4

Printed in Great Britain

Contents

About the Author

Dr Andrew Norman was born in Newbury, Berkshire, UK in 1943. Having been educated at Thornhill High School, Gwelo, Southern Rhodesia (now Zimbabwe) and St Edmund Hall, Oxford, he qualified in medicine at the Radcliffe Infirmary, Oxford.

From 1972–83, Andrew worked as a general practitioner in Poole, Dorset, before a spinal injury cut short his medical career. He is now an established writer whose published works include biographies of Thomas Hardy, TE Lawrence, Sir Francis Drake, Adolf Hitler, Agatha Christie, and Sir Arthur Conan Doyle. He is married to Rachel.

All Andrew Norman's books are displayed on his website andrew-norman.com

List of Illustrations

The Personalities

Southern Rhodesia in the 1950s

Zimbabwe Today

Acknowledgments

The author would like to to thank the Institute for War and Peace Reporting, London; Macmillan Publishers Ltd; Movement for Democratic Change, Harare, Zimbabwe; Pitt Rivers Museum, Oxford, UK; Poole Library, Poole, Dorset, UK; South African High Commission, London; *The Zimbabwean*, Hythe, Southampton, UK.

Thanks also to Pat Bennett; Peter Devlin; Ednam and Joan Dudley; Michael Dragffy; Philip Evans; Gwendoline Flake; Olive Flood; Tom Gillibrand; James Hamilton; Kate Hoey MP; Gillian Lewis; John MacLeod; Bev Nelson; Jean Norman; Jane Savery; Judith Garfield Todd; Archbishop Desmond Tutu; Thomas Norman; and Right Honourable the Baroness Thatcher.

The poems *Quiet Diplomacy* and *Clean Up* and the extract on page 2 from *By Day and By Night* are reproduced by kind permission of Chris Magadza and Poetry International.

I am especially grateful to my beloved wife Rachel for all her help and encouragement.

Author's Note

I have a particular interest in, and concern for Zimbabwe – formerly Southern Rhodesia – having lived there for some years in the late 1950s at the end of the British colonial era. It was long enough for me to gain an impression of the topography of that fascinating and enchanting land and to learn how its people — blacks, Afrikaners (white Afrikaans speakers of Dutch descent), Europeans, coloureds (people of mixed descent, who speak Afrikaans or English as their mother tongue), and others had come together to create what Robert Mugabe described in 1980 as the 'Jewel of Africa'. I still have many Zimbabwean friends, both inside and outside, and both black and white, whose names cannot, for obvious reasons, be revealed.

To those who greeted Mugabe with a tidal wave of euphoria and expectation in 1980 when his country achieved its independence, the present situation seems incomprehensible, for since then, he has brought Zimbabwe to its knees. Was this due to his stupidity and rapacity, or was there a more profound reason, one which impels him to cling to power, no matter what the cost to his country and his people? The author believes that there is a reason, and that only by understanding what it is, is it possible to understand Mugabe and his decision-making processes. The people of Zimbabwe, and of the world at large, deserve to know the truth about Mugabe, and why things in Zimbabwe have gone so terribly wrong.

Preface

As a child, Robert Mugabe benefited from a primary and secondary education at Katuma in rural Southern Rhodesia. He progressed to teacher training college, and then to Fort Hare University in South Africa from which he graduated. Impressively, Mugabe went on to gain six more degrees, some of which he studied for in the most adverse circumstances, from prison, where he was incarcerated for ten long years by his country's white ruling regime.

When Southern Rhodesia became independent from Britain in 1980, Mugabe demonstrated his belief in education by investing heavily in schools, teachers, and equipment. In this way, he raised the literacy rate to about 80 per cent – one of the highest in Africa.

Twenty-eight years later, on 25 February 2008, a Zimbabwean teacher – who, for obvious reasons, preferred to remain anonymous – was interviewed by the BBC World Service. He had just been discharged from hospital. He described how a group of colleagues, both male and female, had decided to hand out leaflets – 'fliers' – at various locations in Harare, protesting about the difficulties the education system was currently experiencing. He was one of a group of four who had taken up their position at Harare's bus station.

The police arrived and demanded to know who had given them permission to act in such a way. They were taken to the ZANU-PF offices, where they were beaten with logs, switches and metallic rods and interrogated by paramilitary personnel for about 1½ hours. The teacher described how he had been beaten on the buttocks by about seven people, in turn. The tissue trauma he suffered as a result caused him excruciating pain. He also described how terrible it was to have to witness others – his female colleagues included – being beaten as well. When asked why he had felt it necessary to make his protest, the unnamed teacher stated:

> The circumstances within the schools were very bad when we were faced with malnourished kids disrupting learning programmes ... There were no learning materials within the schools. It was really the frustration which made me want to demonstrate.

The teacher's experience is born out by Stephen Bevan and other correspondents who reported in The *Sunday Telegraph* on 18 November 2007 that in Zimbabwe: 'Almost a quarter of the teachers have quit the country. Absenteeism is high, buildings are crumbling, standards are plummeting.' At Hatcliffe Extension Primary School in Epworth, 12 miles west of Harare, the children were having to write in dust on the floor because they had no exercise books or pencils. Classrooms were:

> ... filthy and swarming with insects. Instead of chairs the children sit on mud bricks which leave red stains on their tattered, khaki uniforms. Similar scenes can be found across the country.

At the University of Zimbabwe in Harare, it was a similar story. Half the 1,200 lecturers had left during the year, joining a mass exodus of teaching professionals.

Surely, when the teachers of Zimbabwe appealed for help, they might reasonably have expected to be listened to and to have their grievances addressed, particularly by someone with the background in education of Robert Mugabe. But as far as he was concerned, they, like anyone else who dared to complain about the Utopian state which he had created, must expect to be brutally punished. The truth was that Mugabe, once a schoolteacher, was now a tyrant –as such, he had destroyed the very education system which he had helped to create.

Education is not all that Mugabe has destroyed during almost three decades in office; but why? Despite the millions of words written about him in the press, describing him as 'evil', 'a monster', and so forth, no satisfactory explanation for his bizarre, cruel, destructive, and irrational behaviour has been forthcoming.

This book attempts to put Mugabe under the microscope, to explain *just why* this former teacher became a tyrant.

1
Education

Robert Gabriel Mugabe was born on 21 February 1924 at Matibiri village, situated in the Zvimba District of Southern Rhodesia, 50 miles south-west of the country's capital, Salisbury. Mugabe's father, Gabriel Mugabe Matibiri, was a carpenter at the nearby Kutama Jesuit Mission Station. Founded by the Frenchman Jean-Baptiste Loubière in the early 20th century, Kutama was an offshoot of the Chishawasha Mission, established by Catholic pioneer missionaries in 1892. Mugabe's mother Bona, was, 'a devout and pious woman who taught the catechism and the Bible.'[1] Mugabe was the third child of six.

At Kutama, Mugabe attended primary school. In 1934, when he was aged 10, his father abandoned the family and went to Bulawayo – Southern Rhodesia's second city, 200 miles away – in search of work. The Mugabe family was deprived of its breadwinner.

In that year, Father Loubière died and was replaced by Father Jerome O'Hea. The Irishman was an ardent advocate of racial equality, including the provision of education for blacks. O'Hea put his beliefs into practice. At his own expense, he added a secondary school – Kutama College, a technical college – and a teacher training college to the existing facilities at Katuma. He also built a hospital to serve the local Zvimba Native Reserve (which previously had no medical provision at all).

Kutama College, with O'Hea as its first headmaster, was one of the first institutions to offer a high-school education to Rhodesia's blacks. Judging Mugabe to be an assiduous pupil, O'Hea enrolled him at the college. Its motto was 'Esse Quam Videri' – 'To be, rather than to seem.' Was Mugabe all that he seemed? That would become clear later. The Father instructed Mugabe

> ... on the catechism and Cartesian logic [and] gave him a feel for Irish legend and revolution, describing the struggle the Irish had sustained to attain independence from Britain.[2]

Although the prime objective of missionaries like O'Hea was to fulfil their sacred duty to save souls for Christ, they also instilled into their young black charges the ideals of freedom and independence. In other words, they felt no particular allegiance to the prevailing white regime, which could never in its wildest dreams, envisage anything but white rule. The influence of the missionaries, needless to say, angered the majority of white settlers who objected to blacks being educated at all, which gave them ideas 'above their station'.

What was regarded by the whites as the malignant influence of the missionaries was nothing new. In the late 19th century, Cecil Rhodes, Prime Minister of the Cape Colony, had taken a dim view of those who were operating schools and farms in the Glen Grey area of Cape Province. He told the South African Parliament that the 'Kaffir parsons' (native clergy) whom the missionaries were producing, were 'a dangerous class ... [who] would develop into agitators against the government'. He proposed the replacement of the mission schools with industrial schools, 'framed by the government', (where blacks would be taught labouring skills).[3]

Even though his father was absent from home, the young Mugabe had an excellent role model in his mother. As for Father O'Hea, he taught his young pupil to think for himself – at any rate as far as politics was concerned – and to question the colonial system.

O'Hea described Mugabe as having, 'an exceptional mind and an exceptional heart',[4] and in this he was quite correct, though not in the way he imagined. He offered Mugabe a place at the teacher training college and also awarded him a bursary (there being no prospect of financial support from Mugabe's family). Having embraced O'Hea's anti-colonialist doctrine, the next question was whether or not Mugabe would also embrace his mentor's Roman Catholicism.

When, in 1941, Mugabe duly qualified as a teacher, he opted to remain at Katuma and to teach at his former school. He supported his mother and surviving three siblings from his salary of £2 per month (his two elder brothers having already died). In 1944, Mugabe's father Gabriel returned with three more children, borne to him by another woman. He was now gravely ill and when, shortly afterwards, he died, Mugabe found himself financially responsible for six children instead of three!

The following year Mugabe left Katuma to become a primary school teacher at the Dadaya New Zealand Churches of Christ Protestant

Mission School, Shabani. The superintendent of the Dadaya Mission School was missionary RS Garfield Todd, who was soon to make his mark in politics. Like Father O'Hea of Katuma, Todd was a firm believer in full black enfranchisement.

In 1949, Mugabe, now aged 25, won a scholarship to the (all-black) University of Fort Hare in South Africa's Cape Province, described as a 'hotbed of African nationalism'.[5] Here, he came into contact with many black activists: Leopold Takawira (who introduced him to Marxism), Julius Nyerere, Kenneth Kaunda, Herbert Chitepo, Robert Sobukwe and James Chikerema (who was also from Kutama). Mugabe later stated that his 'hatred and revulsion for the system started at Fort Hare … I decided I would fight to overthrow it.'[6]

In Mugabe's early life therefore, O'Hea and Todd sowed the seeds of discontent, and the black activists of Fort Hare instilled in him the basics of revolutionary Marxism. Would Mugabe fight in a non-violent way, like Mahatma Ghandi, or take up arms like the Bolsheviks of 1917?

In 1952, Mugabe, having gained his BA in History and English Literature at Fort Hare and having also joined the African National Congress (ANC), returned to Southern Rhodesia. The ANC was formed as long ago as 1912, an organisation devoted to bringing all Africans together and to championing their rights and freedoms. In that year, he took up a teaching post at the Driefontein Roman Catholic School near Umvuma, 50 miles east of Gwelo. In 1953, he taught at Highfield Government School, Harare Township, Salisbury, and in 1954 at Mambo Township Government School, Gwelo.

From 1955–58 Mugabe, who by now had obtained another degree – Bachelor of Education – this time by correspondence course from the University of South Africa, was employed as a lecturer at the Chalimbana Teacher Training College in Lusaka, Northern Rhodesia. From 1958–60 he was in Ghana – formerly the Gold Coast – teaching at Apowa Secondary School, Takoradi, in the west of the country. Here, he studied for yet another degree – Bachelor of Administration. It was at Takoradi that Mugabe met and fell in love with Sarah Francesca Heyfron – 'Sally' – the daughter of a teacher at the school.

In Ghana, Mugabe met Prime Minister Dr Kwame Nkrumah, who was an inspiration for many black African leaders. With degrees in economics, sociology, theology, philosophy and anthropology, Nkrumah's first publication, *Towards Colonial Freedom*, appeared in 1947. In the same year, he became General Secretary of the new nationalist party, the United Gold Coast Convention. In 1948, urban rioting forced Britain to accelerate the Gold Coast's timetable for devolution. In 1949, Nkrumah created the Convention People's Party whose slogan was 'Self-Government Now'. In 1950, he was imprisoned for inciting a general strike. In the election of February 1951, he was returned as Parliamentary Member for Accra Central. Gold Coast finally achieved independence (the first British African colony to do so) under its new name, Ghana, in March 1957, with Nkrumah as Prime Minister.

Thereafter, at Nkrumah's invitation, educated blacks from various African countries came to Ghana to study, teach, and derive encouragement for their own nationalistic aspirations. Nkrumah

> ... was determined, in particular, to turn Ghana into a launching pad for African liberation: providing a base from which nationalist leaders from colonial Africa could draw support and encouragement.[7]

It is not surprising that Mugabe was drawn to Ghana and Nkrumah; just as O'Hea, Todd, and Fort Hare had nurtured his yearnings for independence, so Nkrumah was now able to demonstrate to him, at first hand, how this could be achieved. Mugabe could also see for himself what the end results of the struggle were; for here in the newly independent Ghana – unlike in Mugabe's own country – the proverbial 'glass ceiling' that had prevented blacks from achieving their full potential had simply ceased to exist. Mugabe now saw blacks being made directors of companies and appointed to the headships of schools and of civil service departments.

During his time in Ghana, Mugabe also attended the Kwame Nkrumah Ideological Institute at Winneba, in the south of the country. 'It was there I accepted the general principles of Marxism.'[8] This statement by Mugabe, made in the late 1950s when he was in his mid-30s, is of great significance. He had decided to embrace Marxism, which denounced capitalism, was committed to a workers revolution, and envisaged the 'dictatorship of the proletariat'. If Mugabe is to be believed, what he desired for Southern Rhodesia was the collectivisation of industry and farms in a country run by a committee of workers. Is this really what he desired, or did he choose Marxism simply because of its diametric opposition to the capitalist system as practised by Britain and the West, and, of course, by the white rulers of his country? Or was there yet another reason?

It would not have escaped Mugabe's notice that in Marxist/Leninist USSR, power resided largely in the hands of one person – Josef Stalin (1879–1953) – and in China, in the hands of Chairman Mao Zedong (1893–1976). Is it conceivable that Mugabe sought such dictatorial power for himself? One day, he would reveal the true reason for his affiliation to the Marxist cause.

2
A Humiliating Life under Apartheid

As already mentioned, before he left Southern Rhodesia for Northern Rhodesia, and later for Ghana, Mugabe began his career in black townships, first at Salisbury and then at Gwelo. What would life have been like for a black person living in Gwelo in the mid-1950s?

Situated in the Midlands region (the area to the east of Salisbury between Matabeleland North and Mashonaland West) Gwelo was Southern Rhodesia's third largest town, with about 46,000 inhabitants, amongst them 8,300 whites. Gwelo was founded in 1894 on a site chosen by Dr Leander Starr Jameson, a colleague of the country's founder Cecil Rhodes. Its name derives from the Ndebele word 'ikwelo' meaning 'a steep descent'. (This may have been a reference either to the slopes of Gwelo's famous 'koppie' – hill – or to the steep-sided banks of the Gwelo river which ran through the town.)

In 1896, the Matabele rose up against the white occupiers of their territory, Matabeleland, in the west of what later became Southern Rhodesia. In the Matabele Rebellion, the inhabitants of Gwelo were forced to *laager.* The word 'laager' derives from the Cape Dutch word 'lager', meaning a camp. (To the early Dutch settlers or 'Vortrekkers', however, it meant the drawing of waggons closely together in a circle and the closing of the intervening spaces with impenetrable thorn bushes. Women, children, and cattle were placed in the centre, the men defending the position against the enemy.) In the Gwelo laager, the townspeople – whose numbers had grown to around 600, since every white person in the vicinity had taken refuge in the town – defended themselves successfully for a period of five months against the Matabele warriors.

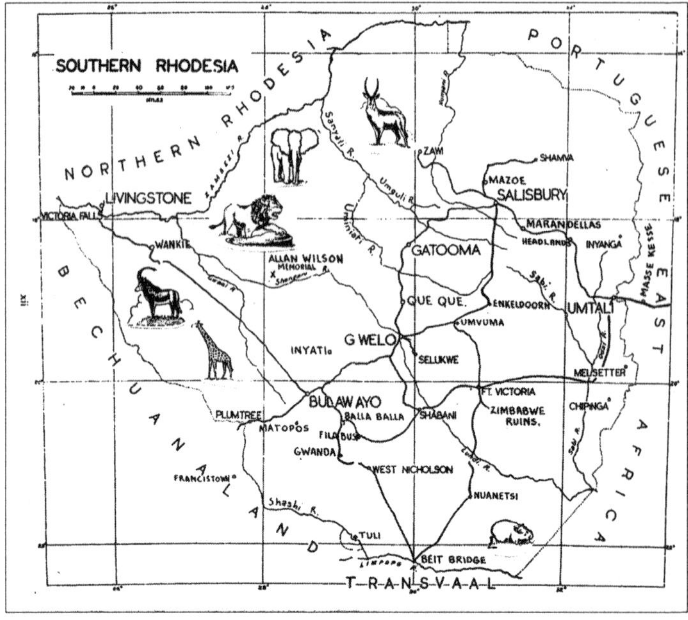

Gwelo, like all Rhodesian towns, was an island in a sea of waist-high grass ('bushveld'); bare in places and dotted with anthills and trees such as: 'umbrella' acacia, mimosa, mopani, wild fig, kaffir-orange, and blue gum eucalyptus. The influence of the Dutch was to be seen everywhere: 'Afrikander' oxen with their humped backs and large horns; bilingual English/Afrikaans road signs, and elegant, gabled buildings. Nearby was the Royal Rhodesian Air Force base at Thornhill.

In Gwelo, the strip roads, consisting of two strips of tarmacadam laid down on the dirt surface to link one town to the next, gave way to fully tarmacadamed streets with deep depressions designed to take away the torrents which fell during the rainy season. On the instruction of Cecil Rhodes, the streets of all major Rhodesian towns had been laid out on a grid pattern, and Gwelo was no exception. In addition, Dr Jameson demanded that they be made wide enough to accommodate a turning ox waggon, complete with its sixteen oxen. The results were most impressive, especially when the trees which lined them (mauve-flowered jacarandas, or red-flowered flamboyants) were in bloom. Gwelo's traffic roundabouts were equally delightful, planted with cosmia, which, when they came into flower, bathed them in colourful drifts of gently swaying pink, mauve and white.

Homes for employees of the Bata shoe factory.

Buildings of note included the Old Stock Exchange (built 1898), the Magistrates Court (1905), and the Town Hall (circa 1905–1910). In the Colonial Style, they would not have looked out of place in an English town. Again, like any English town of a similar size, Gwelo had all the necessary amenities: library, swimming pool, department stores, hospital, post office, municipal buildings and so forth. With minerals abundant in the region, there was heavy industry in the shape of ferro-chrome, iron, and cement works. Furniture and clothing were also produced here, as was footwear by the firm Bata.

On the second Saturday of June each year, the townspeople of Gwelo were pre-occupied with celebrations to mark the Official Birthday of Her Majesty Queen Elizabeth II. This included a march past, followed by speeches from Governor-General Lord Dalhousie, Prime Minister Sir Roy Welensky, and Mayor of Gwelo Mr JR Cannon.

The Member of Parliament for the Midlands District since 1953 and representing the United Federal Party, was Ian Douglas Smith, a farmer from nearby Selukwe. Educated at Chaplin School, Gwelo and Rhodes University, Grahamstown, he had served as an Air Force pilot during World War II in the Rhodesia Squadron. One day, when Robert Mugabe entered politics, Smith would become his principal adversary.

Apartheid, simply the afrikaans word for 'apart' or 'separate', pervaded every aspect of life. The hierarchical structure – of which the blacks formed the lower and far more numerous portion – was evident, for

Preparing for the celebration of The Queen's Official Birthday, Gwelo.

Visit of HM The Queen to Gwelo, 1960.

Selukwe, Ian Smith's birthplace.

example, on Rhodesia Railways, where a black man was restricted to working as a fireman, a platelayer, a general labourer in the mechanical, electrical, signal, or carriage and waggon-repair shops, a ticket seller, or in the parcels office. Only a white man could become a station master, manager, or engine driver. If a black wished to travel by train, he was obliged to sit in a separate 'BLACKS ONLY' carriage on a hard, wooden bench – rather than on an upholstered one, as provided for the whites. Likewise, in Gwelo's hotels – the principal ones being the 'Cecil' and the 'Midlands' – blacks were restricted to working as porters or doormen; in its shops and stores, they would be very much behind the scenes. Black craftsmen, however, were permitted to sell their wares at Gwelo Market. These included carved wooden animals, such as crocodiles and giraffes; miniature buckskin shields, and tablecloths and doilies inlaid with tiny coloured beads.

The 'Blacks Only' buses transported the workers to and from the townships situated on the outskirts of towns and cities. In this vast country, the bicycle was a prized possession, and at Glengarry School, Gwelo, the black employees, of whom there were about a dozen, would club together every month on pay-day and pool some of their money. The person at the top of the list would then visit the cycle shop in Gwelo to purchase a spanking new machine. Newcomers to the staff were placed at the bottom of the list and would have to wait for a year or more.

Street vendor, Bulawayo.

Not all blacks lived in the townships (or in the native reserves that were set aside for them in the countryside), although this was overwhelmingly the case. A few were provided with accommodation by the company or organisation for whom they worked. Also, every white household had servants: one or more 'house boys' or 'garden boys' (an appellation which applied to the worker whatever his age) who were accommodated in a tiny, two-roomed *kia* (outhouse) at the bottom of the master's garden. One of those rooms was used for sleeping, and the other for cooking (using firewood and a cast iron 'missionary pot') and ablutions. Such servants received in addition to their wages a packet of maize meal every day, and a ration of fresh meat twice a week, as did black government employees.

It was forbidden for a black man to address a white woman, unless he was previously known to her. If so, he would call her 'Madam'. White men were addressed as 'baas', or less commonly 'bwana', and white children as 'piccanin madam' or 'piccanin baas'. If a black person wished to visit a town centre, he had to make sure that he carried with him not only his formal identification document or 'pass' – which contained details such as his name, address, fingerprints, photograph, and name of his employer – but also a note from his employer explaining the nature of his business there.

When he walked along the pavement and a white person approached, the black was obliged to give way, even if this meant stepping into the

Blacks being taught building construction skills, Gwelo.

road. If he wished to enter a shop, the likelihood was that he would be confronted with a notice saying 'WHITES ONLY', or in Afrikaans 'SLEGS VIR BLANKES'. Such notices also excluded the coloureds. The same rule was rigorously enforced at the swimming pool (Gwelo's original pool, incidentally, was the first to be built in Central Africa.) Golf, visiting the cinema or 'bioscope', and flying at the Gwelo Flying Club were other pursuits open only to whites.

Gwelo boasted twenty-three schools, providing primary and secondary education for whites, but only primary education for blacks, whose schools were in the townships. There were also two teacher training colleges, one for blacks – Chalimbana, where Mugabe trained – and one for whites. It was at one such primary school for blacks, in a Gwelo township, that Mugabe commenced teaching in 1954.

On the farms, the white farmer would provide for the blacks, at his own expense, a classroom – complete with desks, chairs, books, paper and pencils – and a black teacher. (Where the farm did not possess a schoolroom, lessons would be held out of doors.) The children of farm workers normally received their education free of charge. Outsiders, however, could choose either to pay a two shillings and sixpence per week fee, or to work part-time on the farm and be given their schooling in lieu of wages. As for the white farmer's own children, because of the vast distances involved, they invariably attended white boarding schools, such as Gwelo's Thornhill High and Guinea Fowl.

Fletcher High School.

There were of course far more high schools for whites than there were for blacks. However, on 19 April 1958, the Fletcher High School for blacks opened, situated nine miles from Gwelo. It boasted a library, classrooms (including science laboratories and art and woodwork rooms), assembly hall, dining hall, dormitories for the boarders, and a sick bay. Its Principal was Mr WJF Davies, who was white, as were his members of staff. Its pupils, all immaculately attired in school uniform, were drawn from the upper echelons of black society, being predominantly the sons and daughters of chiefs and tribal elders.

The University College of Rhodesia and Nyasaland, to which all races were admitted, opened in March 1957 at Mount Pleasant, Salisbury. The entry requirements were the same for both blacks and whites, who were taught by the same teachers and studied for the same London University degrees. They also participated jointly in extramural activities such as sport. The accommodation hostels, however, were segregated.

At the university's medical school, there was a strong emphasis on social sciences, with the black population and culture very much in mind. Subjects taught included ancestral worship, spirit possession, propitiation of deceased ancestors, dealings with ngangas (priests, learned in folklore and medicine) and witches. The students also followed courses on the marriage and maternity customs of coloureds, Europeans and Indians; Shona (i.e. Mashona) clans (of which there were five principal ones – the largest being the Karanga and the Zezuru, who comprised fifty per cent of the population of the country); and totems (symbols – usually associated with the name of an animal – which were believed to watch over particular groups). This was the only medical school in Africa to offer such a course.

Gwelo's hospital for blacks was staffed by both black and white doctors. The nurses were trained at the newly-built hospital for blacks in Salisbury which offered a full, state-registered qualification. However, although the hospital was well-appointed and had excellent facilities, large numbers of people were often to be seen waiting around in its spacious grounds – the black population was too big for it to cope. It was not uncommon for a would-be patient to walk many miles in order to be seen at outpatients. Patients diagnosed with leprosy were treated swiftly and for this reason, the disease was in decline. However, severe and chronic cases were cared for at the self-contained leper colony at Fort Victoria. There were also many hundreds of clinics for blacks situated out in the bush. Healthcare was provided free of charge, or 'buckshee' as the locals would say. Despite this, many blacks chose to seek the advice of the local witch doctor, who employed mainly herbal medicines and was extremely influential.

What of the black person who broke the law? Early on a Sunday morning, an employer – such as the headmaster of a local school – might receive an unexpected knock at the door. An extraordinary sight would meet his eyes: that of a dozen or so individuals, each barefoot and attired in red and white-striped T-shirts of varying length – some almost reaching to the knee – and khaki shorts which had clearly seen better days. These were the 'banditi' – convicts, who had broken the law and who were being punished with hard labour. At their head were two soldiers, a sergeant and a corporal, each immaculately attired in the uniform of the Rhodesian African Rifles, and armed with shotguns. All were black. In Southern Rhodesia there was segregation even in the prison system.

The sergeant would then suggest that his men might 'Clear the scrub land, baas?' and if the offer was accepted, the 'banditi' would set to work with their mattocks, removing every single weed in their path and clearing all the stones and rocks. As they did so, they sang.

Whilst his men worked, the sergeant would relax with a smoke, having given his gun to one of the more trustworthy of the banditi. Nonetheless, if anyone tried to escape, that person risked receiving a blast of shotgun pellets to his ankles, or worse.

For a person such as Mugabe, influenced as he had been by Father O'Hea, Garfield Todd, and his colleagues in the ANC, such an environment as existed in Southern Rhodesia – and elsewhere in

Central and Southern Africa – in the 1950s, would have been an endless affront. He would perhaps have admitted that the blacks were not entirely neglected as to health and education, but they were, and would always be, if the whites held sway, second-class citizens. Resentment would therefore have burned away inside him, as he longed for Harold Macmillan's 'Wind of Change' to sweep his country to independence.

Meanwhile, what could he do? He knew that for those who dared to transgress the law in Southern Rhodesia, the penalties could be harsh – something which he would one day experience for himself.

3

On a Collision Course: Black Nationalism and White Procrastination

After World War II, the desire on the part of colonies throughout the world for independence reached a climax. This was true not only for Britain's colonies. In Algeria in 1954, a bitter war started between the National Liberation Front (FLN) and the French colonial army. British Prime Minister Harold Macmillan would describe this phenomenon as a 'Wind of Change ... blowing through this continent ... The growth of national consciousness is a political fact.'[1]

With regard to Britain's colonies in Africa, the British Protectorate of Uganda was well on the way to achieving a peaceful transition to self-government. Likewise in Tanganyika (a United Nations trusteeship governed by Britain) Julius Nyerere and his Tanganyikan African National Union were currently campaigning for independence. In the crown colony of Kenya, there had been great unrest since 1952, when the Mau Mau (Kikuyu secret society) had begun a terrorist campaign to drive white farmers off the land (resulting in the imprisonment of Jomo Kenyatta, leader of the Kenyan African Union, by the British the following year.) It was said by some that 'Mau Mau' stood for 'Moscow African Union', and that the whole continent would soon be subject to a communist takeover. These fears were exploited by die-hard whites who wished to hold on to power.

In the Union of South Africa, the African National Congress – originally called the South African Native National Congress – had been founded in January 1912 by the Zulu, Pixley Ka Izaka Seme, a qualified lawyer, born in Natal and educated at the universities of Columbia, New York, and Oxford, England. The efforts of the ANC notwithstanding, what few rights the blacks possessed were actually being progressively eroded.

Harold Macmillan.

Joshua Nkomo.

In 1948, when the Nationalist Party took office in South Africa with Dr DF Malan as Prime Minister, it began to implement a rigid policy of apartheid with the creation of black independent homelands. In 1950, in response to the passing of the Group Areas Act which segregated blacks from whites, the ANC began a campaign of civil disobedience. This was to no avail. In 1955, eviction of the black population from areas designated as white began. The whites were entrenching themselves more and more deeply, and it was rumoured that a secret organisation of Afrikaners, known as the 'Broederbond', had pledged itself to resist a black takeover to the last.

As for the three British colonies in Central Africa, Nyasaland was a British Protectorate – its Governor from 1949 to 1953 Sir Geoffrey Colby. Leaders of its ANC were Harry Chipembere, Dunduza Chisiza, and Orton Chirwa. Northern Rhodesia was also a British Protectorate, its Governor from 1947 to 1954 Sir Gilbert Rennie. President of its ANC was Harry Nkumbula, with Kenneth Kaunda as its Secretary General. Southern Rhodesia, Mugabe's home country and where he was shortly to play a significant political role, had been a British self-governing colony since 1923. Its Prime Minister since 1933 was Godfrey Huggins. President of its ANC since 1952 was Joshua Nkomo, leader not of Mugabe's Shona people, but of the minority Ndebele (Matabele) people. He was a schoolteacher (with a degree in economics and social science) and a Methodist lay preacher, and had formerly been Secretary of the Rhodesian African Railway Workers' Union.

Since 1953, these three territories had been linked together in a so-called federation. Late in 1948, a delegation from Northern Rhodesia made a visit to London. One of the members of that delegation was Raphael Welensky (known as Roy, who was knighted in 1953.) Born in 1907 in Salisbury, to a Jewish father from Russian-ruled Poland and a mother of Afrikaner stock, he had started his working life as a fireman on Rhodesia Railways. In 1938 he was elected an unofficial member of the Northern Rhodesia Legislative Council, and in 1941 he co-founded the Northern Rhodesia Labour Party. In London, Welensky said his particular concern was 'to find out what Britain's rulers thought about the prospect of closer association between the three Central African territories of Southern Rhodesia, Northern Rhodesia and Nyasaland',[2] which in his view would be an ideal step forward, for the following reasons:

> Northern and Southern Rhodesia had complementary economies: Northern Rhodesia possessed its increasingly prosperous copper-mining industry; whilst Southern Rhodesia had coal, which that industry needed. And across the border from Northern Rhodesia was the then rich, and well-ordered Belgian Congo, which also needed coal. Southern Rhodesia was producing a growing range of consumer goods for which Northern Rhodesia was an expanding market. The two territories already possessed a common currency, common meteorological services, and a single railway system. An apparatus for making co-operation closer already existed in the Central African Council, which had had a permanent secretariat in Salisbury for the past three years.[3]

However, when Welensky suggested to the Right Honourable Arthur Creech-Jones – British Secretary of State for the Colonies in the ruling Labour Government – an amalgamation of Southern and Northern Rhodesia as an initial step, he was met with a flat refusal:

> Do you really believe, Mr Welensky, that any government, either Tory or Socialist, would ever consider either granting Northern Rhodesia a constitution like Southern Rhodesia's, or if there were amalgamation of the two, the kind of constitution which would place the control of several million black people in the hands of a few hundred thousand whites? No government, irrespective of its political hue, would carry out that kind of action today. The world wouldn't put up with it.[4]

This categorical statement by Creech-Jones made it clear that Britain was absolutely and wholeheartedly committed to full enfranchisement for all the occupants of its Central African colonies, prior to these countries gaining independence.

Welensky, however, pressed on regardless, and on 16 February 1949, a conference was convened at the Victoria Falls in order to consider the possibilities of creating a federal association between, not two, but all three territories, Nyasaland included. However, two vital ingredients were missing: no representative from the British Government was present at the conference, nor had any African been invited to it.

In fact, the blacks of Northern Rhodesia and Nyasaland had grave misgivings about the concept of Federation, fearing that if the same 1930 Land Apportionment Act which applied in Southern Rhodesia were to apply in their countries, then the balance of land ownership would change drastically in favour of the whites. In Nyasaland, for example, only 2.5 per cent of the land was owned by whites, and in Northern Rhodesia, white-owned land consisted mainly of a thin, 30-mile-wide strip alongside the country's principal railway line. Sir Stewart Gore Browne, who had represented the interests of Northern Rhodesia and Nyasaland in the Northern Rhodesian Legislative Council since 1938, stated that these two countries were afraid that political progress would be curtailed:

> They were afraid that there would be an extension to their territories of what they regarded as Southern Rhodesia's rigid and reactionary pass laws. Finally, they feared that there would be social and educational discrimination against them.[5]

The positions of whites and blacks on the issue of federation were becoming increasingly polarised. This became clearer at a conference of officials from Britain's Commonwealth Relations Office, the Central African Council, and the three governments in question, held in London in March 1951. The ANC made it clear that it was 'completely opposed to any form of federation'.[6] The views of the ANC were ignored, and in June 1951, when the report of the conference was published, it was unanimous in recommending that a federal system be adopted. Welensky, however, declared that he and Godfrey Huggins (Prime Minister of Southern Rhodesia since 1933) were 'gravely concerned at the break-neck speed with which the British Government wanted to hand over control to the Africans'. What was required, he said, was a step-by-step approach, 'at the rate of which the African showed himself capable of'.[7]

One of those least enamoured of the idea of federation was Dr

RS Garfield Todd.

Hastings Banda of the Nyasaland ANC. A graduate in history and political sciences, Banda was also a qualified doctor who had practised in Britain. With the founding of the Nyasaland African Congress in 1944, he took an increasingly active interest in African politics – attending the Pan-African Congress of 1945 held in Manchester, UK, where he met Kwame Nkrumah of the Gold Coast (later Ghana). Banda now assumed an increasingly pivotal role in opposing federation. In March 1952, as the London representative of the Nyasaland ANC, he addressed a public meeting in Edinburgh called by the World Church Group. A motion

Macmillan and Welensky, Federal Prime Minister of the CAF (Central African Federation).

was adopted, demanding that no scheme for closer association of the Rhodesias and Nyasaland 'should be imposed without the free consent of the African peoples'.[8]

In April 1952, yet another conference was held in London, and once again there was deadlock. Of the six blacks who were included as members – two from each of the three territories – only the Southern Rhodesians chose to attend (one of whom was Joshua Nkomo). Even when the non-attenders agreed to join informal talks, they reaffirmed their 'unanimous opposition to federation'.[9] Nonetheless, despite black opposition, the London conference expressed the hope that the Federation would come into being and attain full membership of the British Commonwealth of Nations (established 1931).[10]

The Federation of Rhodesia and Nyasaland was formally inaugurated on 3 September 1953, with Lord Llewellyn (a former member of Winston Churchill's government) as Governor-General. Sir Godfrey Huggins became Prime Minister of the Federation's interim government, with Welensky as Minister for Transport, Communications and Post. RS Garfield Todd succeeded Huggins and became Prime Minister of Southern Rhodesia. In Northern Rhodesia, the number of African members on the Legislative Council was increased from two to four (out of a total of twenty-six). Meanwhile, Banda relocated to the Gold Coast, where he set up in medical practice in the northern provincial city of Kumasi. The move was undoubtedly inspired by that country's visionary and revolutionary leader Kwame Nkrumah, who in Welensky's words, was 'eager to fulfil his Pan-African dreams as quickly as possible'.[11]

Despite the name 'Federation', there was some variation in the degree of autonomy allowed to the three provinces. Nyasaland, which was the least developed, was ruled by Britain as a crown colony. Northern Rhodesia (although having its own local assembly and legislative council of elected members) was also governed through the Colonial Office in London. Southern Rhodesia, which was the most developed, continued to be self-governing (as it had been since 1923). Matters of common concern to all three territories were presided over by the Federal Parliament in Salisbury.

The motto of the Federation was 'Magni Esse Mereamur' – 'Let us deserve to be great'. To the black majority – and Mugabe undoubtedly shared this view – this white-inspired organisation, whose degree of consultation with them had been only minimal, did not deserve to exist at all. Their representation in government bore no relationship to their numbers, and for them, the whole exercise was an irritating distraction from the main business of the day, which was the attainment of full black enfranchisement and independence.

As time went by it became clear that the Federation, which Roy Welensky had strived so hard to create, was not working out as planned.

> Our chief difficulties lay ... in the two northern territories, in their governments' relations with the Federal Government, and in the increasingly uncooperative attitude of the African leaders – specifically the [African National] Congress Parties – in both territories. The whole [British] Colonial Office system makes them [the Africans] see the issue as

> consisting of two opposed policies, black rule and white rule. They naturally prefer to aim for black rule and hope they will experience this, which they regard as the apotheosis of [United Kingdom] Colonial Office policy. I thought then, and I think now, that much of the responsibility for the Africans' attitude lay with senior Colonial officials, who resented a federal system.[12]

In 1955, in Northern Rhodesia, Nkumbula and Kaunda were each imprisoned for two months for distributing 'subversive' literature.

In July 1957, Welensky bowed to the inevitable and made plans to extend the franchise and enlarge the Federal Assembly. Under the Constitutional Amendment Bill, the total membership of the Assembly was raised from thirty-five to fifty-nine, including forty-four elected members of unspecified race, of whom twelve blacks and three whites would represent African interests. 'The Act also made provision for the eventual abolition of representation merely by race.'[13] The key word here was, of course, 'eventual'.

In that year, 1957, rumours circulated that Prime Minister RS Garfield Todd had engaged in talks with black nationalist leaders without the approval of his parliamentary colleagues. Matters came to a head when members of his Cabinet resigned en masse in protest. The following year, Todd was deposed for exhibiting pro-African traits, and an election brought Sir Edgar Whitehead of the United Federal Party to power.

In 1958, the Electoral Bill – which Welensky admitted was unduly complicated – became law. Nevertheless, he was not displeased. 'The simple fact remains that at one stroke we doubled African representation in the Federal Assembly.'[14] However, this fell far short of full black enfranchisement, which Welensky saw as a potential disaster:

> ... since 1957 we have seen, all over Africa, that one-man-one-vote leads directly to the one-man-one-party dictatorship, which was precisely what we foresaw and, with the lives and livelihoods of the vast majority of moderate and non-political Africans and of Europeans and Asians to safeguard, what we strove to prevent.

Mugabe had not yet appeared on the political scene, but no doubt he followed events closely, even when he relocated to Northern Rhodesia for three years in 1955 to take up his teaching post. What he saw was enormous energy being devoted to the creation of what, for the blacks, was an enormous 'white elephant'. He saw Welensky giving the blacks sops, in the way of a handful of extra seats in parliament. He saw the

British Government advocate black majority rule, but be unwilling to intervene to establish it, and anxious to wash its hands of the problem as quickly as possible. And he looked northwards, with envy and admiration, at Kwame Nkruhma's Gold Coast, as it achieved its independence in 1957.

4

Nyasaland: The Fuse is Lit – Mugabe Returns Home

In July 1958, after 42 years spent in the United States and Britain, Dr Hastings Banda returned to Nyasaland, where, on 1 August, he was elected President-General of the Nyasaland ANC. On 1 December, he attended the all-African Peoples' Conference in Ghana's capital Accra, which pledged him its full support.

Shortly afterwards, Banda was challenged by a journalist as to whether, when the former had declared that he would fight the Federation, he meant by this that he would resort to violence in order to overthrow it. Banda replied: 'I mean [to oppose] not with violence but one can't exclude that if we are not allowed to get out of it.'[1]

In the Southern Rhodesia General Election of February 1958, Sir Edgar Whitehead's United Federal Party won seventeen seats, the Dominion Party thirteen seats, and RS Garfield Todd's United Rhodesian Party, not one. Said Welensky: 'The African nationalist leaders at once vehemently denounced the Constitution which had brought these elections results, and launched a campaign of propaganda and agitation against it.'[2]

Early in 1959, the Nyasaland ANC sent a delegation to London to meet with the British Conservative Government's Colonial Secretary Alan Lennox-Boyd. Welensky, for his part, was highly critical of the British Government, for what he regarded as its duplicitous behaviour:

> Saying again and again that they had faith in the Federation, that they wanted to uphold it and see it successful, they encouraged and assisted the growth of forces absolutely inimical to it ...

Welensky feared that with the upsurge of African nationalism and the demand for immediate independence by British colonies throughout the continent, 'a vast power vacuum was being created, which the communists were only too willing to fill.'[3] He was particularly concerned at the unrest which had accompanied Banda's return to Nyasaland, with cars being stoned and a police station attacked by rioters. This unrest, he attributed to the verbal attacks which the latter and his colleague HB Chipembere, were making on the Federation. An outbreak of rioting in Nyasaland in late February 1959 obliged the Governor, Sir Robert Armitage, to request assistance. Federal troops, including detachments of the 1st Battalion King's African Rifles from Lusaka and 120 European personnel of the 1st Battalion The Royal Rhodesian Regiment were sent by air to Blantyre (Nyasaland) following disturbances at three widely separate points: Karonga, Fort Hill and Rumpi.

When the security forces were deployed, 51 Blacks were killed. The fear now was that events in Nyasaland would have a knock-on effect, and this prompted the Government of Southern Rhodesia to declare a state of emergency on 26 February. The African nationalist parties were banned, and 300 members were imprisoned. However, Nkomo, who was visiting Egypt at the time, escaped capture. He moved to London and did not return home until November 1960, when he was restricted to the Semokwe Reserve south of Bulawayo.

Meanwhile, the situation in Nyasaland continued to deteriorate, with further rioting and six fatal shootings by the security forces. White women and children now began to leave the country by air, and families living in isolated areas were asked by the police to move into the town of Blantyre for their own protection. Finally, on 3 March 1959, Governor Armitage declared a state of emergency throughout the Protectorate. Shortly before the announcement was made, 100 or more of the Nyasaland ANC's senior officials, including Banda and Chipembere, were detained, placed in Federal Custody, and transported to prisons outside the Protectorate. According to the *Rhodesia Herald*, Banda was taken into custody, 'wearing silk pyjamas and a blue dressing gown'. He was imprisoned in Gwelo, Southern Rhodesia.

A Commission of Inquiry was appointed by Britain under the chairmanship of Mr Justice Devlin, to report on the Nyasaland disturbances to the British Conservative Government of Harold Macmillan. When published, it was clear where the commission's sympathies lay – with the blacks:

> Nyasaland is – no doubt temporarily – a police state, where it is not safe for anyone to express approval of the policies of the African National Congress Party.[4]

It also stated that the root cause of the discontent was the dislike of the blacks for the Federation. To Welensky, the Devlin Report was a huge disappointment:

> Since Britain – government, parliament and people – was determined to offload the real responsibilities and obligations of a rulership in Central Africa which she would not hand over to us [the whites], the Federation was to be her scapegoat.[5]

Ndabaningi Sithole.

A vicious circle developed, the hatred now being displayed by many whites towards the ANC members and their leaders equalled by the indignation felt by the blacks at their treatment by the white rulers.

By late 1959, even though most of the ANC detainees had been released, the organisation was still proscribed. However, new names were swiftly created to fill the void. The Southern Rhodesia ANC was reborn as the National Democratic Party (NDP); the Northern Rhodesian ANC became the Zambian ANC; the Nyasaland ANC became the Malawi Congress Party.

The avowed aim of the NDP was not only to achieve political representation, but to abolish the Constitution itself, which it regarded as the source of all discriminatory legislation. One of its leaders was Ndabaningi Sithole who, in his book *African Nationalism*, set out the case for the nationalist cause. A founding member of the NDP was Leopold Takawira, a Catholic teacher whom Mugabe had known from his student days at Katuma. He put it simply: 'We are no longer asking Europeans to rule us well, we now want to rule ourselves.'[6]

Banda was released from prison in April 1960. When he returned to Nyasaland no further violence occurred, and the state of emergency in his country was lifted.

Meanwhile, in May 1960, Mugabe, who no doubt had been following events closely, resigned from his teaching post in Ghana and returned to Southern Rhodesia. For him, sitting on the sidelines was no longer an option. The time had come for him to take a hand. His role now was to galvanise the NDP and, in particular, its youth wing, which would encourage the younger generation to commit themselves to the Party.

5

Mugabe the Publicist

In July 1960, in Southern Rhodesia, two months after Mugabe's return home, Leopold Takawira and three other NDP officials were arrested and charged under the Unlawful Organisations Act. The next day, a crowd of protesters marched eight miles from Salisbury's black suburb of Highfield into the city, in the hope that Prime Minister Edgar Whitehead would meet their delegation. This became known as the 'March of the 7,000'. Whitehead reacted by calling up a battalion of the local territorial militia. The marchers were stopped by riot police at Stoddart Hall in the black township of Harare. The following morning, fifty per cent of the Salisbury District's black labour force boycotted work and joined their comrades at Stoddart Hall, swelling the numbers to 40,000. For Mugabe, this was a great opportunity, and he took it. That afternoon, he addressed the crowd. He told them about the newly independent Ghana, and of his vision that, one day, Southern Rhodesia would emulate the country. This was met with thunderous applause.

Next day, the police moved in. They arrested 130 blacks and wounded many others, some seriously. The following weekend, the unrest spread to Bulawayo, where eleven blacks were shot dead. The government now passed new legislation. The Law and Order (Maintenance) Amendment Act gave the police virtually unlimited powers to deal with the demonstrators. This was too much for the Federation's highly respected Chief Justice, Sir Robert Tredgold. He resigned in protest at the Government's behaviour: 'This bill outrages every basic right. If passed into law, it will remove the last vestige of doubt about whether Rhodesia is a police state.'[1]

In October 1960, Mugabe was elected as the NDP's Secretary for Information and Publicity. He also became editor of *The Democratic Voice*, the NDP's mouthpiece.

Southern Rhodesia's 1961 Constitution was worked out by Whitehead's ruling United Federal Party and the British Government. Under its terms, in the Rhodesian Parliament, the whites were to have fifty seats (the so-called 'A Roll') and the blacks fifteen seats (the 'B Roll'). Once again, therefore, the number of black and white Members of Parliament was hugely disproportionate to the population.[2]

Ian Smith disapproved of the 1961 Constitution because it contained no 'guarantee of our [Southern Rhodesia's] independence in the event of a break-up of the Federation'.[3] Therefore, in early 1962, he resigned the United Federal Party whip in protest and founded the breakaway Rhodesia Reform Party, which within a few months merged with the Dominion Party to form the Rhodesia Front.

In April 1961, Mugabe and Sally Heyfron – who was a convert to Catholicism – were married at the Roman Catholic Church in Salisbury (despite the fact that Mugabe was now an avowed Marxist). That year, the Foreign Office convened a constitutional conference in the city, under the chairmanship of Commonwealth Secretary Duncan Sandys. There, Nkomo, Sithole, and Herbert Chitepo (Southern Rhodesia's first black barrister and advisor to Nkomo) reached agreement on the 1961 Constitution.

This deal was swiftly rejected by Nkomo's NDP executive. As for Mugabe, he described it as a sell-out.

> Europeans must realise that unless the legitimate demands of African nationalism are recognised, then racial conflict is inevitable.[4]

Was this a threat, or was it a statement of fact? The reaction of the government was predictable. In December 1961 the NDP was banned, its funds seized and its leaders prohibited from addressing any public meetings for four months. Within ten days of the ban, Nkomo replaced the NDP with the Zimbabwe African Peoples Union (ZAPU) – in which Mugabe once again fulfilled the role of Publicity Secretary, and also that of Secretary-General. (This was the year that South Africa declared itself a republic and left the Commonwealth.)

In September 1962, the government banned the newly-created ZAPU and placed its leaders under a three-month restriction order; Mugabe was sent into exile – for three months – to a tribal reserve in his home district of Zvimba. The nationalists were also deprived of funds, property, and vehicles, which they could ill afford to lose.

The election of December 1962 was won by the newly-founded Rhodesia Front Party. The electorate had rejected Edgar Whitehead's plans for greater political representation for blacks, and for their integration into schools, hospitals and residential areas which were formerly the sole preserve of whites. Winston Field, formerly of the Dominion Party, now became Prime Minister, with Ian Smith as his Deputy and also his Minister of Finance. In the same month, another constitutional conference was convened to prepare Nyasaland for independence with complete black enfranchisement.

The Law and Order (Maintenance) Act had recently been amended, and the so-called 'hanging bill' now dictated that any person found guilty of throwing an explosive object at a building, whether such a building was occupied at the time or not, would suffer a mandatory death sentence. This, Mugabe described as 'the legalisation of murder'. Consequently, when he returned home three months later from exile, he was arrested, charged with 'making a subversive statement within the hearing of others', and released on bail. Mugabe's wife Sally, had already fallen foul of the authorities when she attacked Britain for abandoning Rhodesia's blacks, including the words 'The Queen can go to hell.'[5] Sentenced to two years imprisonment, she was released on bail, pending an appeal.

In January 1963, restrictions on Nkomo were lifted. He now decided, for obvious reasons, that the time had come for the Executive Committee of ZAPU, Mugabe included, to leave Southern Rhodesia and relocate to the Tanganyikan capital, Dar-es-Salaam. This they did in April. Mugabe was accompanied by Sally, even though she, like him, was awaiting trial for subversion. Also, she was pregnant again, having lost her first child at birth.

On their arrival in Tanganyika, the ZAPU leaders had a setback. Contrary to what Nkomo had led them to believe, they discovered that its President, Julius Nyerere, regarded Nkomo's decision to leave Southern Rhodesia as ill-advised. They therefore returned home, except for Mugabe, who remained in Dar-es-Salaam for the birth of his son Nhamodzenyika (in Shona, the 'suffering country'). On 4 July 1963, a constitutional conference was held at Victoria Falls to prepare Northern Rhodesia for independence.

The Tanganyikan episode convinced some members of ZAPU, Mugabe included, that Nkomo was inept and lacked leadership qualities. Nkomo, for his part, reacted by suspending four 'rebel' members of his Executive Committee, including Party Chairman Washington Malianga, Sithole, Takawira, and Mugabe. On 8 August 1963, as a result of this schism, the Zimbabwe African National Union (ZANU) was created, with the Reverend Ndabaningi Sithole as its President. As for Mugabe, a founding member of ZANU, he was elected in Sithole's absence to be the Party's Secretary-General.

Sithole's ZANU drew its support mainly from the Shona peoples of the south, the east, and the Midlands of Southern Rhodesia, who made up the majority of the country's population. Nkomo's ZAPU, on the other hand, drew support mainly from the Ndebele people of Matabeleland – whose principal city was Bulawayo – and from the impoverished township dwellers of the capital, Salisbury.

Despite the growing political unrest, there were signs that in the Southern Rhodesia of the early 1960s, the apparatus of apartheid was gradually, in tiny but significant increments, being dismantled. For example, a white hotel owner, who had hitherto been obliged to refuse black people the right of admission to his establishment, was now permitted, by a new law which became operative in June 1959, to use his discretion in these cases. As regards shoppers, and railway and airport users, the discriminatory measures whereby blacks and whites were catered for separately were also gradually being abolished. Desegregation was also beginning to occur in some privately owned schools, with black pupils being admitted for the first time. Blacks were now eligible, again for the first time, to compete in the Southern Rhodesia State Lottery, with a first prize of £30,000; also to indulge in betting on horse races, and to purchase European-type beer and spirits.

The Civil Service was becoming non-racial, with parity of income for those who performed equal tasks. Likewise, black doctors and teachers were placed on the same pay scale as their white counterparts. Similar changes were taking place in industry. Trade unions, which had previously existed separately for blacks and whites, now became non-racial with Workmen's Compensation Schemes being introduced, which would give sick or injured employees the same benefits irrespective of their colour. On Rhodesia Railways, a black who passed the appropriate examination at the Railway Training College – situated in the suburb of Raylton, Bulawayo – could now become a conductor, a guard, a driver, or even an administrator.

For more than thirty years, the blacks of Southern Rhodesia had been permitted to own farms on a freehold basis. Now, there were in excess of 6,000 such black farm owners. Blacks, having trained at the Chibero African Agricultural College – 40 miles north-west of Salisbury – found themselves well-equipped to manage their own farms, and to play an increasingly important role in the running of those owned by whites.

White farmers also employed blacks to run their farm shops, which catered for the needs of their local kinsmen. Building societies began to lend money to blacks for the purpose of house-building at the same rates at which they lent to whites.[6]

Would the pace of such changes be sufficient to satisfy the aspirations of the black majority? In particular, would the dismantling of apartheid be followed by similar changes in the political system? If not, would the indignation and frustration of the blacks boil over? Mugabe had foreseen that yes, this was a real danger, and that it could end in racial conflict.

6

Mugabe is Imprisoned: The Demise of the Federation

Having enjoyed the company of his infant child for only three months, Mugabe returned home from Tanganyika in December 1963. He was promptly arrested and remanded in custody to await trial. Meanwhile, rather than allow his wife Sally to return home and face an inevitable prison sentence herself, Mugabe persuaded her to return with their baby to her parents' home in Ghana. The totalitarian, not to say Kafkaesque terms of the order under which Mugabe was detained were as follows:

> Whereas under the terms of Section 50 of the Law and Order (Maintenance) Act, certain powers are vested in me, and whereas certain information has been placed before me and whereas due to confidential information which I cannot reveal, I am satisfied that you are likely to commit acts of violence throughout Rhodesia.

It was signed by Justice Minister Desmond Lardner-Burke. On the 31st of the same month, the Federation of Rhodesia and Nyasaland was dissolved and replaced, in the words of its former Prime Minister Welensky, by:

> ... three small states, in two of which [Northern Rhodesia and Nyasaland] there is rapidly being established the domination of one race, one party and one man – and this in the name of democracy. [However, he did admit that] In both these countries this kind of authoritarianism is at present probably the only method of achieving some degree of political stability, since the way of ordered and reasonable process has been rejected.

And then, with foreboding:

> There is no room in a black-dominated country for whites who will not knuckle under to their new and angry masters, as has already been made quite clear in the two northern territories.[1]

Despite this, Welensky remained guardedly optimistic, as far as Southern Rhodesia, a self-governing colony within the British Commonwealth, was concerned. 'We must keep steadily on the road of construction and reconciliation.'[2]

Dr Banda became Prime Minister of Nyasaland in 1963: a position in which he continued after the country achieved its independence the following year, under a new name, Malawi. In Northern Rhodesia, Kenneth Kaunda, a cabinet minister since 1961, became President when the country achieved independence in 1964 as the Republic of Zambia. That year, Kaunda said of Zambia:

> We would like an opposition that is non-tribal, non-racial and non-religious (by non-religious of course, I mean one that is not based on any religious grouping). A sweeping victory at any given election is no mandate to legislate against the formation of an opposition.[3]

In August 1964, Mugabe was sent to Salisbury's maximum security prison, 'until this order is revoked or otherwise varied by me [Lardner-Burke]'. There would be no trial, and Mugabe would spend the next decade confined in various prisons. About 150 ZAPU and ZANU leaders were also detained, including Nkomo, who was sent to a detention centre at Gonakudzingwa in the south-east of the country. His period of imprisonment would also last for ten years, just four months less than Mugabe's.

Now ZANU and ZAPU, each anxious to bolster support, and by intimidation if necessary, became increasingly hostile to one another. Mobs rampaged through the black townships of Salisbury and through some of the tribal trust lands (formerly known as native reserves); there were assaults, bombings, arson and stonings.

During his years of imprisonment Mugabe endured many hardships: one of the greatest of all, to this inveterate reader and accumulator of university degrees, was being denied access to written material. From Salisbury, Mugabe was transferred to Wha Wha Prison near Gwelo, where conditions were equally harsh, and subsequently to Sikombela Prison, Que Que, where prisoners were expected to build their own houses,

Mugabe with Kenneth Kaunda to his left.

with walls and floors of *daga* – a mixture of mud and straw – and roofs of thatch. It was a measure of Mugabe's growing stature that his fellow-prisoners did him the honour of building his house for him. Meanwhile, in the outside world, the whites were planning their next move.

To many in his Rhodesia Front Party, Southern Rhodesia's Prime Minister Winston Field looked like someone who was liable to sell the white Rhodesians down the river. They believed that he had not applied sufficient pressure on the British government to recognise that country's right to full independence – under white rule, of course. By contrast, his colleague Ian Smith, was made of sterner stuff. For example, Smith had constantly avowed that, in his lifetime, there would never be black majority rule.

In June 1964, Sithole joined Mugabe in prison. In August, Smith, faced with continuing internecine strife between ZANU and ZAPU, banned both organisations and arrested their leaders.

In prison, Mugabe was determined to keep his mind occupied, and those of his comrades too. When restrictions on reading matter were lifted, he took upon himself the role of headmaster, and using books donated by charities such as Christian Aid and Christian Care, established a school. In this, he was assisted by his fellow-prisoners; those with some education being enlisted to teach those with little or none.

Harold Wilson's endless attempts to reach an accommodation with Ian Smith ended with UDI.

In the autumn of 1964, Harold Wilson's Labour Party came to power in Britain. In Southern Rhodesia, Smith gathered together a council (*indaba*) of black chiefs — almost all of whom were government employees — and announced that all 622 of them were in favour of the country's independence under the 1961 Constitution. Anxious to avoid a white breakaway, Wilson flew to Salisbury that October. In a final attempt to find common ground, he talked to Smith, and also to Nkomo and Sithole, who were released from prison for the occasion. However, the two nationalist leaders, although they initially declared that they would accept the 1961 Constitution, changed their minds and rejected it.

In May 1965, Smith felt sufficiently confident to call a general election. He achieved total victory for his Rhodesia Front Party, which won all 50 of the white seats in Parliament. Someone who did not support Smith, however, was former Prime Minister RS Garfield Todd. Seen by

Ian Smith. Prime Minister of Rhodesia 1964–79. In May 2000 the 81-year-old's cattle and maize farm in central Zimbabwe would be invaded by about 50 people, pegging out plots. 'I'm not worried, I have more black friends than Mugabe,' was his reaction. 'There is no politics on my farm.'

the Smith regime as a dangerous liberal and a threat to the white regime, he, together with his family, had been placed under house arrest at his ranch at Hokonui, 110 miles from Bulawayo.

In his continuing negotiations with Wilson, Smith fought for the same objective which had led him to resign from the Federal Government in 1961: a guarantee from Britain of Southern Rhodesia's full and unconditional independence. Wilson offered to set up a Royal Commission to consider the matter. At the same time, he made it clear that he would not be bound by the findings of this Commission, and that the terms for independence must be, 'acceptable to the people of Rhodesia as a whole'.

When, on 29 October 1965, Wilson made the tactical error of announcing publicly that he would not use military force even if Smith broke away from Britain unilaterally, Smith took this as a green light to do exactly that.[4]

Meanwhile, at Sikombela Prison, security was suddenly tightened. When Mugabe asked the reason why, his worst fears were realised: for on 11 November 1965, Smith had made a Unilateral Declaration of Independence (UDI). The Governor, Sir Humphrey Gibbs, now dismissed Smith and his Cabinet, and the British Government assumed formal responsibility for Southern Rhodesia, in name only.

Garfield Todd was one of the few whites who believed – rightly so, as it transpired – that Southern Rhodesia post UDI would be a disaster. He applied to leave the country for Scotland, in order that he might educate the British public about what he perceived to be the iniquities of white rule in Rhodesia. His application was refused. He was arrested, detained in police custody, and then returned to house arrest. Britain's response to UDI was to impose sanctions, culminating in an oil embargo, which the Rhodesians managed to circumvent by importing oil through Mozambique rather than South Africa, as they had done hitherto.

Sympathetic warders smuggled letters in and out of Sikombela Prison, enabling Mugabe to keep in contact with ZANU Chairman Herbert Chitepo, who was busy in Lusaka, Zambia, establishing guerrilla bases and preparing for battle. Mugabe's warning of the inevitability of racial conflict was about to come true.

In May 1966, guerrillas from ZANU's military wing – the Zimbabwe African National Liberation Army (ZANLA), composed mainly of Shona – infiltrated Rhodesia from Zambia, and raided a farm near Hartley, 50 miles from Salisbury, murdering the farmer, Johannes Viljoen, his wife Johanna, and their 3-year-old son. All the insurgents were subsequently killed by the Rhodesian security forces. This incident led the government to transfer the ZANU executive – Mugabe included – and thirty other ZANU detainees, to the remand section of Salisbury's Central Prison. This is where Mugabe had begun his sentence, and this is where he would remain for another eight years.

Smith and Wilson held further talks; this time, aboard the Royal Navy's HMS *Tiger* in Gibraltar. They were unsuccessful. Britain now invoked a United Nations mandate and used its Royal Navy to blockade the Mozambique port of Beira – the terminus for Rhodesia's vital oil. On 7 November 1966, George Thomson, Wilson's Minister without Portfolio, flew to Salisbury for talks with Mugabe, Takawira and Sithole. Here, he was asked by Mugabe a perfectly legitimate question: why had Britain failed to act against an illegal seizure of power by the white regime?

In Salisbury Prison, more relaxed conditions enabled Mugabe – whose appetite for knowledge was insatiable – to study for London University degree examinations by correspondence course. 'I do it for myself and Zimbabwe [he refused to call the country 'Southern Rhodesia'] because I know that one day we both will need these degrees.'[5] Astonishingly, he acquired three such degrees to add to the four which he already possessed, including a law degree and a BA in Administration.

Late in 1966, an inspector of Rhodesian police arrived at Salisbury Prison in company with Mugabe's sister. Mugabe was told that his son Nhamodzenyika, then aged three, had died of cerebral malaria at his wife's parents' home in Ghana. He was inconsolable. He begged the prison governor to grant him parole to attend the funeral in Accra, the Ghanaian capital. His request was refused.

The years 1967–68 saw further incursions of guerrilla groups into Rhodesia from Zambia, but they met with little success. In October 1968, Smith and Wilson held talks aboard HMS *Fearless* – again in Gibraltar. Once more, their talks proved fruitless. Meanwhile, Sally Mugabe was not idle. Funded by the Ariel Education Initiative — which was devoted to excellence in teaching and learning in inner-city schools — she moved to London to study for a degree in Home Economics at London University's Queen Elizabeth College.

In 1969, Smith introduced a new Republican Constitution, drawn up unilaterally and without the participation of the British government. This decreed that the basis by which blacks could achieve representation in parliament was, henceforth, to be determined solely by the amount of tax that they contributed to the exchequer. Smith knew full well that the contribution to the exchequer made by blacks was currently less than one per cent of its total receipts, and that therefore, in his own words, this new Constitution, 'sounded the death knell of the notion of majority rule[6] [and] would entrench government in the hands of civilised Rhodesians for all time'.[7] Smith also introduced the Land Tenure Act which stated, again, 'for all time', that the areas of the country set aside for whites and blacks would each total 45 million acres; the remaining 6 million acres to be designated as national parks and game reserves.

The Reverend Ndabaningi Sithole had condemned himself in Mugabe's eyes when, in 1969, he renounced the armed struggle against white Rhodesia. Now in Salisbury Prison, the authorities alleged (although he denied it) that they had caught Sithole in the act of throwing oranges over the wall to party members posing as visitors. Concealed in these oranges were written instructions for the assassination of Prime Minister Smith. Sithole was brought to trial in January 1969, charged with conspiracy to murder, found guilty, and sentenced to six years imprisonment. Even prior to this, Sithole's supporters had become disaffected, and when the presidency of the party was put to the vote, he was deposed and Mugabe was declared leader of ZANU.

In June 1970, when a Conservative government came to power in Britain, led by Sir Alec Douglas-Home, it reached agreement with the Smith regime on the basis of Smith's 1969 Constitution. However, when Douglas-Home visited Salisbury, and the African leaders were released from prison in order that he might hear their views, he was told by Mugabe, in no uncertain terms, that the blacks rejected the 1969 Constitution and intended to fight for their rights. A commission was sent to Zimbabwe by Britain, chaired by Lord Pearce, It reported that 'The people of Rhodesia as a whole do not regard the proposals [Smith's] as a basis for independence.' Douglas-Home's agreement with Smith was now at an end.[8] In the same year, Takawira died in prison, of undiagnosed diabetes.

Over the next two years, Mugabe was encouraged to hear that in neighbouring Mozamibique, nationalist guerrillas of FRELIMO (the Front for the Liberation of Mozambique) were making slow, but sure progress in their war against the Portuguese colonial government. By 1972 they controlled large areas of the north of the country. ZANU's military wing, ZANLA, made common cause with FRELIMO and, backed by Communist China, Yugoslavia and Romania, it began to operate from FRELIMO-controlled territory inside Mozambique. In December 1972, ZANLA guerrillas attacked a Rhodesian farmhouse in the Centenary District near Salisbury. A truck which came to investigate was blown up with a land mine, which killed its driver – a white corporal. South Africa came to Southern Rhodesia's aid by dispatching a large contingent of combat 'police' to bolster the country's defences.

Nkomo, for his part, established a military wing for his party, ZAPU, in Zambia. Backed by the Soviet Union and East Germany, and consisting mainly of Ndebele people, this wing was named the Zimbabwe People's Revolutionary Army (ZIPRA).

When, in the early 1970s, Rhodesia's prison authorities clamped down by placing restrictions on study materials for detainees, Mugabe circumvented this. He enlisted the help of his wife Sally, and sent references to her in London for those documents which he required; whereupon she meticulously tracked them down, transcribed them by hand and posted them to him.

In 1972, Garfield Todd and his daughter Judith, were imprisoned. Todd was subsequently confined, once again, to his Hokonui ranch; Judith spent the next seven years in exile.

Mugabe with Samora Michel.

In 1974 in Portugal, there was a military coup, after which a new democracy was created with General Autó Ribeiro de Spinola as its first president. The decision was made to withdraw Portuguese troops from Mozambique and Angola, and to grant these colonies independence as quickly as possible. This gave Southern Rhodesia's blacks further hope. It also made South Africa's president John Vorster realise that soon he would have black-dominated African states as his neighbours, with the attendant threat of guerrilla incursions into his country. Seeing Southern Rhodesia as another source of political unrest, Vorster now commenced a dialogue with Zambia's Kenneth Kaunda, aimed at persuading Smith to end hostilities with ZANU and ZAPU; to release all political detainees in Southern Rhodesia and to restore the legality of its nationalist parties.

On 1 November 1974, Sithole was suspended from ZANU. Mugabe and former ZAPU Chairman Malianga, were released to attend talks in the Zambian capital Lusaka, designed to prepare the way for a Rhodesian settlement. Also in attendance were leaders of the Front Line States: Kenneth Kaunda of Zambia, and Samora Machel, leader of Mozambique's nationalists (both of whom had supported Nkomo and Mugabe in their war efforts, and permitted guerrilla bases to be established on their territories); Julius Nyerere of Tanzania (formerly Tanganyika and independent since 1961), and Seretse Karma of Botswana. As the talks progressed, Mugabe shuttled back and forth from Salisbury Prison to

Lusaka by air; on one occasion being reunited with his wife Sally, for the first time in ten years.

The talks did not run smoothly. Mugabe was angry with Kaunda who had arranged a détente with Vorster. Kaunda, in turn, was angry about the constant bickering that was taking place between the two nationalist leaders Mugabe and Nkomo. Additionally, both Kaunda and Nyerere found it difficult to accept Mugabe as leader of ZANU, and not Sithole.

By declaring UDI in November 1965, Ian Smith had not only defied the British Government, he had also attempted to hold back the tide in a world where the currents were running ever more powerfully against colonialism. The outcome, as Mugabe had so rightly predicted, was now inevitable – racial conflict in the shape of a civil war.

Can Mugabe be criticised for becoming leader of a guerrilla army? Smith's behaviour, in declaring UDI, was certainly outrageous, and Mugabe had judged correctly that he and the whites would never relinquish their hold on power voluntarily – they would cling on to the bitter end. Mugabe could argue, justifiably, that he had fought long and hard to prevent some shabby deal being struck between Smith, his more moderate black political opponents (Joshua Nkomo included) – all of whom he despised – and the British Government. He could also argue justifiably that if Southern Rhodesia's neighbours, Northern Rhodesia and Nyasaland, were on the verge of achieving their own independence, then why should Southern Rhodesia be denied hers?

Indian leader Mahatma Gandhi would undoubtedly have approached the problem in a non-violent way. However, Gandhi was not the historical norm. Mugabe was no Gandhi, and for him, the only way to address the problem was to take up arms.

7

Freedom and Exile

In November 1974, Smith, under further pressure from South Africa, ordered the release of Mugabe, Nkomo and Sithole from prison. By now, of all the nationalist leaders in all the countries of the Commonwealth, Mugabe had the unenviable distinction of having spent a longer time in prison (eleven years) than anyone else. (Nelson Mandela would serve 27 years, but he had begun his sentence in 1962 – the year after South Africa had withdrawn from the Commonwealth.) Nkomo now took the opportunity to travel widely in Africa and Europe in order to promote ZAPU's goal of black majority rule.

The effect of those long years of imprisonment on Mugabe can only be imagined. Favourite pleasures were denied him: watching sporting events, especially cricket; listening to traditional Shona music and to such favourites as Bing Crosby, Elvis Presley and Pat Boone, and also to classical music. Of far greater significance was that in his absence, both of his children had died. Although there must have seemed to be no end in sight to his incarceration, his spirit had remained unbroken and his ambitions undiminished.

In March 1975, Sithole was brought before a special tribunal and charged with leading an unlawful organisation (ZANU), but in the middle of his trial, President Vorster of South Africa intervened, telling Smith that to proceed with the case would damage the chances of peace. Sithole was released.

The following month, Sithole attended the Organisation of African Unity's (OAU) Foreign Ministers' Conference in Dar-es-Salaam. Here, he met with Nkomo and Bishop Abel Muzorewa, joint founder with the Reverend Canaan Banana of the United African National Council

(UANC) whose slogan was 'No Independence before Majority Rule'. Educated in the United States, the 50-year-old Muzorewa was Bishop of the United Methodist Church. His UANC was in favour of a peaceful internal settlement of the country's woes, as opposed to an armed confrontation.

The 49-year-old Mugabe, now a free man, realised that as a political activist in Southern Rhodesia he was liable to be re-arrested at any moment. Therefore, in March 1975 he and ZANU Secretary-General Edgar Tekere left secretly for Mozambique. Three months later the guerrilla war in Mozambique ended, and the country gained its independence from Portugal with Samora Machel as its first president. However, with the release of Sithole, the authorities in Mozambique were disinclined to accept Mugabe as the leader of ZANU. The FRELIMO leaders, therefore, placed him in protective custody. When restrictions on Mugabe were finally lifted, he was free to take up residence in the Mozambique port of Quelimane; from where he visited the north of the country and also Tanzania, where military training camps for ZANU's forthcoming war effort were being established.

Meanwhile, Nkomo, Sithole and Muzorewa continued to pursue the policy of détente with Smith, which Mugabe so despised. They failed to reach agreement with him at a conference held at the Victoria Falls in August 1975.

In November 1975, ZANU (pro-Marxist with Chinese-trained and equipped forces) and ZAPU (pro-Soviet and armed by the Soviets) put aside their differences and joined together to form the joint Zimbabwe People's Army (ZIPA) with nine representatives from each on the council of its high command. ZIPA, however, collapsed after brutal internal clashes between the two rival groups. Then, in late November 1975, there was a factional split within ZANU itself, Sithole breaking away to create the moderate ZANU (Ndonga) Party.

After taking her Degree in Home Economics in London, Sally Mugabe commenced work for the Runnymede Trust — devoted to the fight against social injustice and racial discrimination. She also took the opportunity to lobby British Members of Parliament on behalf of Zimbabwe's black nationalists.

In January 1976, almost 1,000 guerrillas infiltrated Southern Rhodesia's eastern border from Mozambique, and attacked white farms. The Rhodesians responded by drafting all men over the age of 38 for compulsory military service. At the end of that month, Mugabe travelled to London, where he accused Zambia's President Kaunda of arresting his men and imprisoning them, or restricting their movements.[1]

In February 1976, the leaders of the Front Line States visited Mugabe at Quelimane, to be told by Nkomo that negotiations with Smith had failed. A few days later, the Rhodesian Air Force attacked a village just inside Mozambique. Machel responded by closing the border and giving Mugabe permission to use his northern province of Tete as a base for mounting military strikes on Southern Rhodesia. A month later, in an effort to enlist help from the outside world, Mugabe visited Switzerland where the Kampfendes Afrika Organisation presented him with 10,000 Swiss francs as a donation to the cause.

In the spring of 1976, Machel installed Mugabe and his wife Sally in a Portuguese-style villa situated near the coast at the capital Maputo (formerly Lourenco Marques). This would be their home for the next four years. When Russian arms dealers insisted that Mugabe recognise Nkomo as the overall leader of the black nationalists, Mugabe responded by seeking more arms from his main supplier – China.

Guerrilla infiltrators into Southern Rhodesia began intimidating black farm workers, ordering them to abstain from work, and ambushing their company buses if they refused. The Rhodesian military responded by disguising themselves as FRELIMO soldiers and attacking the guerrilla camp at Nyazonia, 35 miles inside Mozambique. Here, they killed 670.

Alarmed by the support of the Soviets and the Chinese for the guerrilla forces, US Secretary of State Henry Kissinger became involved, visiting Central Africa several times in the summer of 1976. By then, the Front Line States had universally recognised Mugabe as the leader of ZANU. At a meeting with the Front Line presidents that September, Mugabe accused Nkomo of pulling his ZAPU troops out of the war and leaving all the fighting to ZANU's military wing, ZANLA.

Three weeks later, Smith, under heavy pressure from Kissinger, made a speech to the nation, accepting the principle of majority rule.[2] In October, the Patriotic Front – a military alliance between Mugabe's ZANU and Nkomo's ZAPU – was created. Mugabe now went from strength to strength. Photographs appeared in the Mozambique press, depicting him with President Machel who, despite his initial misgivings, now gave the ZANU leader his full backing.

On 9 October 1976, Mugabe and Nkomo issued a joint statement rejecting Kissinger's proposals under which an interim government would be established in Southern Rhodesia. Instead, their aim was to pursue an 'armed liberation struggle until the achievement of victory'.[3]

At a conference held in Geneva, Switzerland on 28 October 1976, attended by Nkomo, Smith, Kissinger, and Mugabe, the latter declared that the new country which he envisaged would, '... draw on the socialist systems of Mozambique and Tanzania'.[4] He conceded that:

> One cannot get rid of all the trappings of free enterprise. After all, even the Russians and Chinese have their petit bourgeoisie.

So Mugabe was having second thoughts about Marxism. It is hardly surprising that he expressed his objection to Kissinger's plan because it envisaged that both the army and the police would remain under the control of the whites. No agreement was reached as to the timescale for independence, nor to the form that the proposed interim government was to take.

Sally Mugabe had taken a home economics degree – with its emphasis on food and nutrition – in order that she might be of greater service to the people of Zimbabwe. She now busied herself by assisting black nationalist guerrilla forces in northern Mozambique and in Tanzania, together with refugees from Southern Rhodesia who had fled there. She also travelled to Scandinavia, where she raised funds to purchase food, clothing and medicines for the cause.

With Tongogara now released from prison and in command of ZANU once more, the guerrillas began to attack 'soft' targets in Southern Rhodesia, such as St Paul's Mission at Musami, where seven missionaries were killed, and a store in Salisbury, where 11 were killed and 76 injured by a bomb. Meanwhile, volunteers for ZANU poured into Mozambique from Southern Rhodesia at the rate of 1,000 per month.

In March 1977, Mugabe complained that insufficient material assistance was being given by the Front Line States – members of the OAU (Organisation of African Unity) – and 'friendly socialist countries' to the Patriotic Front, which he claimed had 'a well-planned strategy that would bear immediate results if more aid was forthcoming'.[5] On 31 August, he gained the final seal of approval when his Party's Congress-in-exile proclaimed him President of ZANU.

New Anglo-American initiatives for a settlement – put forward by Britain's Foreign Secretary Dr David Owen and by the United States UN Ambassador Andrew Young – were denounced by Mugabe as, 'imperialist manoeuvres [that] pay lip-service to the principle of majority rule'.[6]

Emnity between Mugabe and Nkomo increased, when Mugabe learned of a secret meeting in late September between Nkomo, Smith, and Kaunda. Mugabe, already suspicious of Nkomo, believed the reason that the ZAPU leader had failed to commit all his forces to the war effort was because he was hoping to make a behind-the-scenes deal with Smith.

At the end of October 1977, Britain's Field Marshal Lord Carver arrived at Dar-es-Salaam, where the idea of a United Nations peace-keeping force to police a cease-fire in Southern Rhodesia was mooted. However, in the absence of any detailed plans for a handover of power, both Mugabe and Nkomo rejected it. Smith, still anxious to reach agreement with moderate leaders Sithole and Muzorewa ('puppets' of the Smith regime, as Mugabe called them), now struck at Chimoio deep inside Mozambique, in an attempt to crush Mugabe's guerrilla army.

In November 1977, a war-weary Smith, under pressure from the United States, reached agreement on majority rule with Muzorewa and Sithole, whereby the whites would retain 28 of the 100 parliamentary seats, and control of the security forces and treasury. However, talks in Malta in January 1978, between Mugabe, Nkomo, Owen, and Young, again foundered on the question of who was to control security during the period of transition between white and black rule. That April in Dar-es-Salaam, Mugabe told Cyrus Vance, Secretary of State in President Carter's US Administration, that during the transition, his forces – which numbered about 40,000 compared to Nkomo's 20,000 – must have the dominant role. Meanwhile, on Zimbabwe's eastern border, guerrillas continued to drive white farmers from their farms.

Talks between Prime Minister Smith and Bishop Muzorewa (for the United African National Council – UANC,) Senator Chief Jeremiah Chirau (for the Zimbabwe United Peoples Organisation,) and the Reverend Ndabaningi Sithole (for the African National Council), but not Mugabe or Nkomo, led to the signing of the Internal Constitutional Agreement, whereby full enfranchisement was promised by 31 December 1978. On 3 March 1978, it was agreed that an executive council made up of Muzorewa, Sithole, Chirau, and Smith would conduct the affairs of state prior to elections. A new constitution was drafted, according to which ten seats in the Senate (Upper House of Parliament) and 28 seats in the House of Assembly (Lower House), were reserved for the white minority.

Mugabe, who (like Nkomo) felt that this arrangement still fell far short of what was required, travelled widely to gain support for his cause: he visited Moscow, Vietnam, North Korea, and Cuba where Fidel Castro agreed to send military advisors to Mozambique, Angola and Ethiopia to train his men. So despite the signing of the Internal Constitutional Agreement, the violence continued.

In a ZANU attack on the Elim Mission Station in the Vumba Mountains on 23 June 1978, eight British missionaries and four children (one a baby) were barbarously murdered. When this drew worldwide condemnation, Mugabe attempted to blame the atrocity on Rhodesia's elite Special Forces Unit – the Selous Scouts. In Lusaka that August, Nkomo again met Smith without Mugabe's knowledge. This left Mugabe furious, both with Nkomo and with Zambia's President Kaunda for condoning the meeting.

Now it was Nkomo's men who were to incur the opprobrium of the world at large by shooting down with heat-seeking, ground-to-air missiles, two Viscount Air Rhodesia passenger aircraft and massacring the survivors. The Rhodesian Air Force retaliated by bombing guerrilla bases in Zambia.

In November 1978, Mugabe visited Italy, where Italian political parties had organised a 'Southern Africa Solidarity Conference'. Here, he astonished his audience by giving it a lecture on how Italy had been transformed from an empire into a democratic state. Could it be that Mugabe, having flirted with Marxism, was now embracing western-style democracy?

In December 1978, ZANU achieved its most spectacular success by blowing up Salisbury's largest fuel depot, causing a five-day fire that destroyed a month's supply of fuel. Hundreds of guerrillas now positioned themselves in tribal trust lands near Salisbury ready to attack. Mugabe christened 1979 as 'The Year of the People's Storm'. He was undoubtedly winning the guerrilla war and was adamant that 'The final blow, the most decisive knock-out by the people's mailed fist, must be effected soon.'[7]

Elections, the first to be held in the country under the principle of universal suffrage, were held in April 1979. They brought victory to Muzorewa's UANC, despite the fact that ZANU had nullified his support in rural areas by forcibly keeping his supporters away from the polling stations. Meanwhile, in Britain, on 3 May, Margaret Thatcher's Conservative Party came to power with a large majority.

On 1 June 1979, Muzorewa became both Prime Minister and Minister of Defence and Combined Operations in the Government of National Unity, with Ian Smith as his Minister Without Portfolio. Black Africa, the United Nations and the rest of the world did not recognise the new regime.

At the beginning of August 1979, Mugabe sent as his representative to the Commonwealth Conference at Lusaka Edgar Tekere, with a hostile message, not only for the white Rhodesians, but also for his black nationalist rivals; and for Thatcher herself. In it, he referred to 'the evil settler racist armed forces ... the treacherous Muzorewa [and Thatcher's] racist mind'.[8] Thatcher, however, struck back by reiterating the British Government's long-held commitment to black majority rule, albeit with a permanent white representation in Parliament. Meanwhile, a transitional period was envisaged which would be managed, 'under British Government authority with Commonwealth observers'.

Finally, in September 1979, all parties, including Nkomo, Muzorewa, Smith, Thatcher and her Foreign Secretary Lord Carrington, met in London for the Lancaster House Conference. Mugabe attended the conference only with reluctance, after pressure from Kaunda and from Machel, who threatened to withdraw their support for him in the face of damaging raids by the white Rhodesians on guerrilla bases in their countries.

8

The Lancaster House Conference and Beyond

The Lancaster House Conference – held between September and December 1979 – was attended by three delegations: that of the United Kingdom; that of Nkomo and Mugabe, and that of Bishop Muzorewa, which included several whites – Ian Smith among them.

At Lancaster House, it was agreed that Bishop Muzorewa should stand down as Prime Minister of Southern Rhodesia, and that Christopher Soames should take charge as British Governor prior to elections. (Lord Soames was a Tory cabinet minister, a former ambassador to France, and the son-in-law of the late Sir Winston Churchill.) Mugabe and Nkomo agreed to a proposed new Constitution, whereby blacks would have 80 seats in the new parliament and whites 20. In the interim, the Governor would keep law and order by using the existing Rhodesian Police Force, whose commander was General Peter Walls. Mugabe was utterly opposed to this. 'If ever there was a case for a UN peace-keeping force, this was it,' he declared, and he went further: 'Unless Lord Carrington relents, we will pack our bags and go back to war.'[1]

Although Kaunda and Carrington were of the same mind – that the Patriotic Front must be included in any settlement – Carrington also demanded pledges from both Mugabe and Nkomo that cross-border raids from Zambia and Mozambique into Southern Rhodesia must cease. Mugabe, in turn, demanded a two-month military truce prior to the election campaign, and indicated he would accept the presence of a Commonwealth peace-keeping/monitoring force of several thousand men to police it. He feared that although the black military had been given equal status with white, the Rhodesian forces might take the opportunity of the cease-fire to herd his troops into detention centres

The signing of the Lancaster House Agreement. Seated, left to right: Dr SC Mundawarara, Bishop AT Muzorewa, Lord Carrington, Sir I Gilmour, Mr JM Nkomo, Mr RG Mugabe.

and destroy them 'within days'. Mugabe made two further demands: that the white forces return to their bases well before his own troops emerged from the bush, and that there be guarantees that all South African forces present in Rhodesia be withdrawn.

There was another clause in the Constitution with which Mugabe was not fully satisfied:

> The British government will require the governments of countries bordering on Rhodesia to make arrangements to ensure that externally-based forces do not enter Rhodesia.

To this, Mugabe requested that the words 'including South Africa' be added. The request was refused. The deadlock was finally broken when it was agreed that a proposed Commonwealth monitoring force of 600 personnel would be increased to 1,200.

In the final plan, the white Rhodesian forces were allotted 47 operational bases within Southern Rhodesia for their troops, and the Patriotic Front 14. Now came another sticking point, in that none of the Patriotic Front bases were to be in the central Midlands region – the economic heartland of the country — where the majority of the whites with their settlements and vast farms were concentrated.

An urgent message was delivered to Mugabe from Machel. Speaking on behalf of the Front Line States, he told Mugabe that the war was over, and that he must accept the terms offered. Machel had realised that if the Lancaster House talks failed, then his country would be in danger of attack from the white Rhodesians, who might well invade northern Mozambique in order to deal Mugabe's forces a final, mortal blow. Faced with this ultimatum from Machel, Mugabe had no choice but to acquiesce.

Under the terms of the Lancaster House Agreement, Zimbabwe – as Southern Rhodesia was now to be called – would become a sovereign republic, and Zimbabwean citizenship would be automatically guaranteed for every person who had been a citizen of Southern Rhodesia immediately before independence. Zimbabwe's Constitution would be its supreme law. Its president, to be elected by Members of Parliament, would be Head of State and Commander-in-Chief of the defence forces. He would hold office for six years; after which time he would be eligible for re-election for one further six-year term only.

The Senate (Upper House) would consist of 40 members: 10 white, 14 black, 10 to be elected by the Council of Chiefs, and six to be nominated by the President on the advice of the Prime Minister. The House of Assembly (Lower House) would consist of 100 members: 20 white and 80 black. Any citizen over the age of 18 would be eligible to vote.

The Constitution's Declaration of Rights granted everyone a right to life; to personal liberty; to freedom from slavery and forced labour; to freedom from torture and inhumane treatment; to protection of privacy of home and other property, and to protection under the law. There would be the right of freedom of conscience, whereby it would be forbidden to interfere with anybody's philosophical or religious belief; freedom of expression; freedom of assembly and association, and freedom of movement. There would be protection from discrimination by reason of race, tribe, place of origin, or political opinion.

The Declaration of Rights also stated that there would be freedom from deprivation of property. This of course was of particular relevance to the white farmers. Annex D of the Agreement dealt with the Pre-Independence arrangements, and Annex E dealt with the Cease-Fire arrangements.

The Constitution was enacted on 6 December 1979; the signatories being Lord Carrington, Sir Ian Gilmore, Bishop AT Muzorewa, RG Mugabe, JM Nkomo, and Dr SC Mundawarara of the Muzorewa delegation. Mugabe had therefore put his signature to a document guaranteeing democracy in the new Zimbabwe and full civil rights for all its citizens.

The question now was whether ZANU and ZAPU should fight the forthcoming election together, or separately. Nkomo, who anticipated that he would become the first black prime minister of Rhodesia, believed that they should present a united front, but Mugabe and his Central Committee thought otherwise, and decided to go it alone. Mugabe's ZANU would contest the election under a new name – ZANU-PF (Patriotic Front). The only dissenting voice in ZANU was Tongogara, who argued strongly for a joint campaign.

On the return journey from London, Mugabe stopped at Dar-es-Salaam to meet with the leaders of the Front Line States. Here, he received a setback. President Nyerere made it known that, in his view, the split between ZANU and ZAPU would divide the vote and play into the hands of Bishop Muzorewa.

On Christmas morning 1979, Mugabe arrived back at Maputo, Mozambique, where President Machel and most of his Cabinet met him at the airport. Nkomo sent a delegation from Zambia, also urging that the two parties join together. Tongogara agreed, and he also supported Nkomo in his desire to be leader of the proposed new Patriotic Front. However, Tongogara's pleadings were to no avail, and he was dispatched to the guerrilla camps in Mozambique to explain the Lancaster House Agreement to the guerrilla leaders. One hundred miles north of Maputo he was killed in a road traffic accident. Although there were suspicions that he might have been assassinated, Mugabe gave the appearance of being genuinely shocked by the event.

Meanwhile, Lord Soames demanded that Mugabe should not be permitted to return home until his political opponents, who had been purged from ZANU two years previously and were currently languishing in prison in Mozambique, were released. Mugabe, who regarded this as an excuse to delay his return, sensed a conspiracy, and declared that he had, 'lost every ounce of faith in the British government'. Nevertheless, prompted by Machel, he agreed to Soames' demand.

After their five-year sojourn in Mozambique, the Mugabes, and 100 or so of his ZANU-PF supporters, took the 90-minute flight from Maputo to Salisbury, where tens of thousands of followers were waiting to greet them.

There were enormous problems to be faced. One million people had been uprooted from their homes, and it was now too late in the year for them to sow the seeds for the following harvest. Schools serving half a million children had been closed because of the war. There were scarcely any doctors to serve the rural areas. At a press conference, Mugabe reiterated ZANU-PF's vision for the future:

> The State of Zimbabwe must be truly democratic. In other words, there must be a complete reversal of the situation where you have equals and unequals, superiors and inferiors, whites and blacks.

When he arrived at Highfields township, an estimated 200,000 people sang his praises, held portraits of him aloft, and gave him a five-minute standing ovation.

The cease-fire continued to hold. Meanwhile, Lord Soames' thinly-stretched Commonwealth monitoring/peacekeeping force was dispatched to await the arrival of the guerrillas into their designated assembly camps. However, by mid-January 1980, there were reports that some of Mugabe's men had breached the terms of the Lancaster House Agreement. Of the 3,000 or so who had returned from Mozambique, only 1,000 had presented themselves at the assembly camps, the remainder being still at large. A further disquieting fact was that whereas Nkomo's guerrillas had joined the Rhodesian forces to form an integrated army, Mugabe's had not. This was because Mugabe feared if he won the forthcoming elections scheduled for 27–29 March then his opponents would stage a military coup. He was assured by General Walls that this would not be the case. Coming from the man who said of the black militants' demand for equal status that it was 'nonsense ... If anybody shoots at us we will stop them shooting any more,' the assurance was hardly convincing.

Smith had no intention of permitting Mugabe to prevail in the election. In January 1980, he told PK van der Byl (one of his former government ministers and also a minister in Muzorewa's interim government) that 'The plan was clear, and in keeping with what had been the objective at Lancaster House: bringing together the anti-Communist parties in order to ensure that Mugabe and his Marxist-Leninists did not win.'[2]

On 1 February 1980, the Mugabes moved into 27 Quorn Avenue, Mount Pleasant – a mainly white suburb of Salisbury – with their own armed bodyguards and a white policeman to patrol the grounds. Nevertheless, on 6 February, a grenade was thrown at Mugabe's house. It exploded but there were no casualties. On 10 February, another attempt was made on his life.

When an issue of the left-wing newspaper *Moto* appeared, containing an article which attacked Mugabe and suggested that he was 'a psychopath suffering from paranoia', the Mambo Printing Press that produced it was blown up. Mugabe had undoubtedly arranged or condoned this destruction – an indication that the ZANU-PF leader would brook no criticism. So much for the guarantee of freedom of expression, as enshrined in the Lancaster House Agreement.

9

Independence; Doubts About Mugabe

Prior to the March 1980 election, Ian Smith continued to have grave reservations about Mugabe, and he warned British Conservative Foreign Secretary Lord Carrington, that 'through the use of his machine of intimidation, which was ready to move into top gear when the command came [he] would win a majority of seats'.[1]

Smith's fears were confirmed by the eight British electoral advisors, who, in their interim report on the progress of the election campaign, stated that more than half of the non-white population of Rhodesia was being intimidated by Mugabe's guerrillas and supporters. In five of the country's eight electoral districts, conditions for free and fair elections did not exist. On the other hand, the advisors had found little evidence of intimidation by the 23,000-strong army of Bishop Muzorewa — the so-called Rhodesian Security Force Auxiliaries — although there were rumours of this, particularly in the Salisbury township of Harare. Soames' message to Mugabe was that the intimidation must stop. 'The country [must] get a clean bill of health. I look to you.'

Evidence from the Cease-Fire Commission also showed that the vast majority of the 207 breaches of electoral procedure reported were attributable to Mugabe's forces. As one of the Commission's advisors said: 'Eight black parties are trying to carry out a political campaign, and one [ZANU-PF] is conducting a paramilitary exercise.'

At 9 a.m. on 4 March 1980, Sir John Boynton, Chairman of the Election Staff, announced that of the 100 contested parliamentary seats, Mugabe's ZANU-PF had won 57; Nkomo's ZAPU had won 20 (all in Matabeleland); Smith's Rhodesia Front 20; Muzorewa's United African National Congress 3. As for Sithole's ZANU (Ndonga) Party, it came away empty-handed.

When the results were declared to loud cheers, Mugabe stood motionless, while his wife Sally embraced everyone around her. In a televised speech, Mugabe sought to allay the fears of the white community:

> There is no intention on our part to use our majority to victimise the minority. We will ensure there is a place for everyone in this country.

For businesses there would be no wholesale nationalisation: white civil servants would be guaranteed their jobs and pensions; the rights of farmers and householders to property would be respected; to all the people of South Africa there was an offer of peaceful coexistence. 'Let us forgive and forget,' Mugabe stated. 'Let us join hands in a new amity.'[2]

Mugabe fulfilled his promise to make General Peter Walls the supreme commander of the armed forces, and to make two whites members of his first Cabinet. David Smith, a former Rhodesia Front minister would become Commerce Minister, and Dennis Norman, former President of the white farmers' union, the Agriculture Minister.

Although Nkomo was made Home Affairs Minister, he realised that his presence in Mugabe's Cabinet was purely symbolic, and he was now being side-lined. He was, as he put it, nothing more than a 'china ornament sitting in the showcase'.[3] Nkomo was also aggrieved that his Party had been allocated only four of the 23 available Cabinet seats.

At midnight, 17/18 April 1980, in the presence of Prince Charles and several world leaders, the British flag was hauled down and replaced by the flag of Zimbabwe, with its stripes of green (for the land), gold (for the minerals), red (for blood spilled), and black (for the people.) Her Majesty the Queen sent a personal message to Mugabe:

> It is a moment for people of all races and all political persuasions to forget the bitterness of the past and to work together to build a better future for their country and for their citizens.[4]

Mugabe concurred. 'The wrongs of the past must be forgiven and forgotten.'

The first President of Zimbabwe – the last British colony on the African continent to gain its independence – was the Reverend Canaan Banana. Former Prime Minister RS Garfield Todd was appointed Senator by Mugabe. (He served in the Senate until his retirement from public life in early 1985.)

At the independence celebrations, held in Salisbury's football stadium, Nkomo and his wife maFuyana, were snubbed; this time excluded from the VIP enclosure. In Nkomo's words, the couple were 'hidden away like something to be scared of. I am the father of Zimbabwe. What have they done to me?' Of Mugabe, he said: 'He was my friend. We fought the war together. We've worked together. We've brought our forces together. And now Robert has cut me off.'[5]

Outwardly, at least, a surprising cordiality existed between Mugabe and Smith, who at the opening of Parliament on 15 May 1980 walked into the debating chamber side by side. This was despite the fact that Smith's government had imprisoned Mugabe for 11 years without trial, prevented him from attending his son's funeral, and described him as, 'the apostle of Satan'.[6] Smith, who continued to run his 6,000-acre farm at Selukwe, now described Mugabe as, 'a model of reasonableness[7] ... He behaved like a balanced, civilised Westerner, the antithesis of the communist gangster I had expected'.[8]

Despite Mugabe's assurances, many whites remained apprehensive, and for a number of reasons. For example, having misused funds donated by Nigeria to purchase the South African company that controlled the majority of Zimbabwe's newspapers, Mugabe proceeded to dismiss their white editors and replace them with government appointees. Since then, a constant stream of propaganda from ZANU-PF has emanated from the radio, television and press, containing frequent references to the 'racist whites'. The result was that, in 1980 alone, some 17,000 people – one tenth of the white population – left the country, taking their skills with them.

To the unbiased observer, the dichotomy between Mugabe's reassuring rhetoric, where he talked of harmony, reconciliation, a fair, non-racially based society, clearly intended for public consumption, and what was happening on the ground – brutality, intolerance, and intimidation – was emerging.

Britain sent military advisors to help the former guerrilla forces and Rhodesian army integrate into a new Joint High Command under General Walls. This was no easy task. Nkomo's ZIPRA army of some 20,000 men had been recruited mainly from Matabeleland. They spoke in Sindebele and had been trained as a regular force. Mugabe's ZANLA army, on the other hand – which was twice as large – was derived mainly from Shona-speaking areas and had been recruited as a guerrilla force. (The history of the two was bloody, the Matabele having dominated the majority Shona in the 19th century, before the arrival of Rhodes.) To make matters worse, a disillusioned Walls retired from his post as Head of the new Joint High Command in July 1980, declaring that he had no faith or confidence in Mugabe's leadership. Finally, when Walls admitted that he had attempted to persuade the British Government to declare the election of 1980 null and void, Mugabe had no choice but to send him into exile.

To South Africa, Mugabe offered the hope of peaceful coexistence. 'We are against apartheid,' he said, and although Zimbabweans 'have a duty to assist our brothers and sisters' no nationalist guerrilla bases would be established on Zimbabwean territory.[9] However, Mugabe's and Nkomo's former guerrillas presented a problem, in that far fewer of them could be integrated into the new national force than the thousands that wished to join.

Meanwhile, tensions between ZIPRA and ZANLA grew. In September 1980, when 17,000 guerrillas were moved into temporary accommodation at Chitungwiza, 15 miles from Salisbury, fighting broke out between Mugabe's and Nkomo's men. In November, street battles in Bulawayo between the two rival factions claimed 55 lives, with more than 200 people injured. These incidents gave Mugabe the excuse to relieve the guerrilla units of their weapons and to demote Nkomo, in January 1981, to the insignificant post of Minister in Charge of the Public Service. The following month, Smith warned Mugabe that 'The Matabele [Ndebele] [are] suspicious of his Government's intentions to create a one-party state that would eliminate the Matabele nation.' Mugabe replied that the suspicions of the Ndebele were unwarranted. When Smith pressed the point, and expressed the view that the fears of the Ndebele were real, he 'detected indifference' on Mugabe's part.[10]

As Britain began to finance a programme of land redistribution – whereby whites would be recompensed over and above the price when they sold their farms to blacks – the USA provided Zimbabwe with a three-year aid package worth $225 million. Following the Zimbabwe Conference on Reconstruction and Development (ZIMCORD) held in March 1981, other international donors provided £636 million.

The South Africans, who now had three avowedly Marxist states — Zimbabwe, Angola and Mozambique — as their immediate neighbours, began recruiting a network of spies and saboteurs inside Zimbabwe in order to destabilise the regime. They also took control of RENAMO (the Movement for National Resistance.) This was an anti-Communist political and military organisation which had been created by Southern Rhodesia's Central Intelligence Organisation in order to oppose Mugabe's ZANLA forces in Mozambique. The effects were soon felt. In July 1981, the South African Joe Gqabi, the ANC's chief representative in Zimbabwe, was assassinated in Salisbury. A month later, the armoury of the Inkomo Military Barracks near Salisbury was blown up.

Now, RENAMO forces in Mozambique began to attack lines of communication between Zimbabwe and the Mozambique port of Beira, including the oil pipeline.

Mugabe responded in August 1981 by inviting North Korean military advisors to Zimbabwe to train a new unit, the 5th Brigade – the Shona name for which was 'Gukurahundi' ('the wind that sweeps away the chaff before the spring rains'). Drawn almost entirely from former ZANLA troops who were loyal to him, this brigade would be placed under Mugabe's personal control. The real reason for its creation – to tutor men in the techniques of interrogation, torture, and murder – would soon become apparent. In the same month, Mugabe offered white Bulawayo-based lawyer David Coltart (born in Gwelo in 1957) the following assurances:

> As you are no doubt aware, we, in government, intend to establish a non-racial society based on equality – and the promotion of the well-being of all our people in accordance with our socialist principles [not Marxist]. It is in this connection that we have adopted the policy of reconciliation whereby our people must put aside the hatreds and animosities of the past and approach the future in a positive and constructive frame of mind and with commitment and dedication to the all round development of the new Zimbabwe. As we struggle to rebuild our country out of the destruction of war we look to young people like yourself to assist us to achieve our objective of establishing a prosperous and harmonious and humane society in this country. I hardly need to remind you that this is as much your home as it is ours.[11]

The activities of the 5th Brigade would soon give the lie to Mugabe's letter.

In December 1981, seven people were killed when a bomb destroyed the ZANU-PF headquarters in Central Salisbury. Mugabe believed, probably correctly, that 'counter-revolutionary elements ... acting in collusion with South Africa' were behind the attack.[12] In the same month, white MP Wally Stuttaford was arrested, imprisoned, tortured, and accused of plotting to overthrow the government. When a review tribunal declared Stuttaford's imprisonment to be illegal, the government ignored it, and also failed to pay the damages awarded to him by the court.

On 7 February 1982, Mugabe announced that a cache of arms had been discovered on Ascot Farm near Bulawayo in Matabeleland – the heartland of Nkomo's ZAPU Party. This was not altogether surprising; it being the case that both ZANLA and ZIPRA had cached large quantities of weapons on their return to Zimbabwe at the cessation of hostilities in 1980. However, Mugabe alleged that this was evidence of a planned military coup and, as more farms were raided and more arms caches were discovered, his language grew more vitriolic. He also pointed out that Ascot Farm belonged to a ZAPU-owned company, one of whose directors was Nkomo.

This gave Mugabe, who had already marginalised Nkomo, the perfect excuse to dismiss him and his ZAPU colleagues from government, and also to seize his Party's businesses, farms and properties. Having Nkomo in the Cabinet, said Mugabe, was 'like having a cobra in the house. The only way to deal effectively with a snake is to strike and destroy its head'.[13]

Furthermore, Nkomo's former ZIPRA soldiers – whom Mugabe called 'dissidents' – were dismissed from the Joint Military Command. Finding themselves unemployed and destitute, they returned to their homes in Matabeleland and indulged in an orgy of violence: murdering some 600 civilians, including ZANU-PF members, whites (mainly farmers and their families) and foreign tourists. South Africa added fuel to the fire by establishing bases in northern Transvaal where these former ZIPRA combatants were trained to infiltrate Matabeleland and provoke civil unrest. However, it was not only Nkomo's men who were discontented; for thousands of Mugabe's former ZANU guerrillas who had also been dismissed from the army were similarly directionless and destitute.

On 18 April 1982, Salisbury was renamed Harare, probably after the Shona chieftain Nehawara. (Prior to independence, Harare was the name of the black area now known as Mbare.) In July, at Zimbabwe's main air force base at Thornhill near Gwelo, 13 aircraft were sabotaged. Several senior air force officers were arrested – including Air Vice-Marshal Hugh Slatter – and tortured until they confessed to involvement in the crime. At their trial in August 1983, Slatter and five of his fellow officers were acquitted and released, only to be immediately re-arrested by the government; another early example of Mugabe's disdain for the rule of law. In November, Ian Smith's passport was confiscated because of his 'political bad manners and hooliganism'. He had criticised Zimbabwe whilst in Britain and in the USA. Meanwhile, the white exodus continued.

On 5 March 1983, Nkomo's home was attacked. He was away at the time, but his driver and two domestic servants were killed. Mugabe commented: 'The dissident party and its dissident father are both destined not only for rejection but for utter destruction as well.'

'Dissident' was to become a favourite word in Mugabe's vocabulary, a 'dissident' being someone who did not agree with him. Nkomo fled the country, first to Botswana and then to Britain. This pattern of persecution by Mugabe of his political opponents continued with the detention of Bishop Muzorewa, an outspoken critic. Muzorewa was detained from November 1983 until September 1984, when he fled to the USA. In July 1984 the Rhodesia Front re-branded itself the (multi-racial) Conservative Alliance of Zimbabwe.

Mugabe's determination to crush all opposition is clarified by this statement, made in the same year:

> The one-party state is more in keeping with African tradition. It makes for greater unity for the people. It puts all opinions under one umbrella, whether these opinions are radical or reactionary.[14]

Such a nonsensical piece of self-justification would not have been written by Hitler. Here it was, the truth from Mugabe at last. He simply desired that his party, with himself at its head, should have total power. This had been his objective all along – the creation of the one-party state.

Mugabe achieved this objective on 22 December 1984, when Nkomo, who had by now returned home, signed (doubtless under duress) a 'Unity Document'. Zimbabwe now became a one-party state — that party, of course, being ZANU-PF.

The parliamentary elections of June 1985 were a charade, as ZANU-PF youth brigades (modelled on Communist China's revolutionary Red Guards) did all they could to intimidate the electorate, as the police stood idly by. Nevertheless, Nkomo's ZAPU held all 15 seats in Matabeleland. Ian Smith also proved that he still had considerable support, when his Rhodesia Front Party captured 15 of the 20 seats reserved for whites. ZANU-PF gained 64 seats, which gave it a substantial overall majority in Parliament.

When the human rights group Amnesty International described the practice of torture in Zimbabwe as 'widespread' and 'persistent', Mugabe dismissed its findings as 'a heap of lies'. He was equally dismissive of a damning report on the same subject by the Catholic Commission for Justice and Peace, and even of the findings of two of his own Government Commissions.

On 12 September 1986, a bill was introduced in Parliament ordering the suspension of Ian Smith for failing to support the imposition of sanctions against the white South African regime. Smith now left politics and retired to his farm at Selukwe, now renamed Shurugwi.

In April 1987, Mugabe banned ZAPU and jailed its officials – including five of its MPs. In that year, he chose, unilaterally, to abrogate various clauses in the 1979 Constitution. The post of Prime Minister was abolished, and on 31 December, he was sworn in as Executive President. This made him Head of State, Head of Government and Commander-in-Chief of the Defence Forces. He now had the power to dissolve Parliament and declare martial law; to control all senior posts in the police, civil service and military; and to run for as many terms of office as he wished. Following independence, Mugabe had taken care, periodically, to renew the State of Emergency, which gave the government authority to detain people without trial, or even those who had been tried and acquitted by the courts. He also abolished the clause that reserved 20 of the 100 parliamentary seats for whites, thus reducing the strength of the parliamentary opposition to a single seat: that of the tiny ZANU-Ndonga Party (founded by the Reverend Ndabaningi Sithole).

Edgar Tekere – once Mugabe's staunchest ally and friend – had became an outspoken critic of his policies. 'A new class of masters' had emerged, he said, which had:

> ... hijacked the revolution. I fear we are heading towards a dictatorship ... Democracy in Zimbabwe is in intensive care and the leadership has decayed.[15]

When Mugabe's wife Sally fell ill and was diagnosed with a serious kidney complaint, he revealed that he could be as ruthless in private as he could be in public. 'I knew the life of my first wife was going to be short, so I knew how to prepare for life after her.' Accordingly, in 1987, he embarked on a clandestine affair with Grace Marufu, one of his office secretaries, who was forty years his junior and married with a son. 'I wanted children, and this is how I thought I could get them.'[16]

In 1988, Mugabe had his first child by Grace. She was named Bona, after Mugabe's mother. That September, the US-based Hunger Project awarded Mugabe the Africa Prize for 'Leadership for the Sustainable End of Hunger'.

In April 1989, Tekere launched a new party – the Zimbabwe Unity Movement (ZUM) – which gained immediate support from the black townships of Harare, Bulawayo, Mutare (formerly Umtali) and from students of the University of Zimbabwe. Tekere condemned himself in Mugabe's eyes by joining forces with the Conservative Alliance of Zimbabwe – the direct descendant of the Rhodesia Front. Mugabe's response was predictable, and the ZUM was subjected to the same intimidation and persecution that ZAPU had previously suffered.

In Gweru (formerly Gwelo), the authorities even went so far as to alter the electoral boundaries in order to give ZANU-PF a better chance (a classic example of the American invention, gerrymandering). Not surprisingly, when Tekere challenged Mugabe for the presidency in 1990, he acquired only 17 per cent of the votes.

Mugabe took further steps to consolidate his already overwhelming political strength, by increasing the number of Members of Parliament to 150. Of these, 20 were appointed by the President, and 10 were chiefs — who were elected by a council of chiefs whose appointments Mugabe controlled.

Those opposition parties which contested the 1990 Parliamentary Elections did so more in hope than in expectation. They included Bishop Muzorewa's United Parties (an amalgamation of his former United African National Council and the Forum Party); the Reverend Ndabaningi Sithole's ZANU-Ndonga Party; Austin Chakaodza's Popular Democratic Front, and Edgar Tekere's Zimbabwe Unity Movement. Mugabe won 117 of the 120 contested seats. This was the year that Nelson Mandela was released from prison in South Africa. It was also the year that Grace bore Mugabe a second child, Robert. Despite the adulterous relationship, Mugabe continued to attend Sunday Mass at Harare's Catholic Cathedral.

In 1991, ZANU-PF formally deleted all references to 'Marxism', 'Leninism', and 'scientific socialism' from its Constitution. (Though Mugabe continued to be known as 'Comrade'.) For Mugabe and for his Party members, plundering the country's wealth for their own self-aggrandisement had become a far more attractive proposition than promoting egalitarianism amongst its people.

Meanwhile, Mugabe continued to play his habitual, duplicitous game of presenting one face in public and another in private. In October 1991, he hosted the Summit Conference of Commonwealth Leaders, and signed the Harare Declaration of Democratic Principles, which committed Zimbabwe to full 'western' freedom and democracy. Mugabe's wife Sally died on 27 January 1992.

In the elections of April 1995, ZANU-PF went one better than the last time around, capturing 118 of the 120 seats. One of the Party's candidates was Margaret Dongo, Member of Parliament for Harare East, who was an ex-guerrilla, a founding member of the War Veterans' Association and a member of ZANU-PF's Central Committee, and of its Women's League. In the 1995 elections, Dongo had stood for the constituency of Harare South where she knew that she had massive support. But she had been outspoken in Parliament, defending democracy and marginalised groups in the country. When, to her amazement, she failed to gain the seat, she asked both the Registrar General and the Electoral Commission to investigate the matter. When they both refused, she appealed to the High Court, which found (massive) irregularities in the proceedings and ordered that another election be held the following November. This time, disgusted with ZANU-PF, she stood as an independent candidate and was duly returned to Parliament. Clearly, the previous vote had been rigged. Dongo was disgusted by the way Mugabe and his Party were lining their own pockets:

> I would have died for Mugabe, but once [his followers] got their farms, houses and limos, they forgot about the people who put them there.[17]

In October 1995, the Reverend Ndabaninge Sithole was arrested and charged with arms possession, terrorism, and conspiracy to murder President Mugabe (in an attack on his motorcade, which had taken place the previous August.) On 17 February 1996, he was remanded in prison, and then released on bail of Z$100,000.

On 17 August 1996, Mugabe married Grace Marufu in the tiny church at Katuma Mission, where he had lived as a boy. Archbishop Patrick Chakaipa, head of the Catholic Church, officiated at the ceremony – albeit reluctantly. Unlike Sally, Grace showed no interest in charitable causes. She preferred a life of luxury, and was not averse to feathering her nest by speculating on the housing market at the government's expense.

In December 1997, Sithole was sentenced to two months imprisonment for conspiring to murder Mugabe, but released on bail. He relocated to the USA where he died three years later. It is doubtful whether there was any truth in the charges.

10

Morgan Tsvangirai and the Movement for Democratic Change

In December 1997, there was a general strike in protest at the raising of taxes by Mugabe to cover the cost of paying pensions to war veterans. The strike was organised by 47-year-old Morgan Tsvangirai.

Tsvangirai was a former miner who had become Vice-President of the Zimbabwe Mine Workers' Union. A one-time supporter of ZANU-PF, he had obtained a diploma in Trade Union Studies at Cresta College, Nottingham, England. On his return to Zimbabwe in 1988, he was appointed Secretary-General of the Zimbabwe Congress of Trade Unions (ZCTU) which represented 27 unions — its 400,000 members made up one-third of the country's workforce.

Mugabe's reaction to the strike was predictable and brutal. Tsvangirai was severely beaten and rescued only in the nick of time by his security guards, as his attackers attempted to throw him out of the window of his tenth-floor office. Tsvangirai would become Mugabe's main political opponent.

On 11 September 1999, the people of Zimbabwe found a new voice when Tsvangirai launched the Movement for Democratic Change (MDC) – with himself at its head. The launch was held before a crowd of 15,000 people at Harare's Rufaro Football Stadium, where 19 years previously Zimbabwe's Independence Day celebrations had been held. In June 2000, elections would be held, and MDC supporters would then be able to demonstrate their opposition to Mugabe.

In November 1999, Mugabe proposed that he should be permitted to hold office for another ten years, in breach of the terms of the 1979 Constitution. When in February 2000 he held a referendum on the issue, the 'No' vote was 54.7 per cent. Mugabe ignored the referendum, and the Constitution was amended in his favour. In fact, afterwards, he went as far as to express his pleasure at the way the referendum had been conducted.

> Especially remarkable was the rare sense of order, maturity and tolerance during the process. The world now knows Zimbabwe is a country where opposing views can file so singly and so peacefully to and from the [polling] booth. I have every confidence that the forthcoming general elections will be just as orderly, peaceful and dignified.[1]

As usual, he was making plans in private to bludgeon the electorate into submission, next time around.

On 1 April 2000, the National Constitutional Assembly, an alliance of church and civic groups, human rights activists, lawyers and journalists organised a 'March for Peace' through the centre of Harare. Over 7,000 people, including blacks and whites of all classes, expressed their opposition to political intimidation and to the invasion of white-owned farms by Mugabe's war veterans. This was a peaceful demonstration, until about 200 war veterans – who had assembled at ZANU-PF headquarters under the supervision of their leader Chenjerai Hitler Hunzvi – attacked and savagely beat the marchers with clubs and iron bars in full view of the riot police, who failed to intervene.

On 15 April, a car containing three MDC supporters was bombed by ZANU-PF. Talent Mabika, a 23-year-old MDC official, and Tichaona Chiminya, Morgan Tsvangirai's 38-year-old personal driver, were burned to death. Mugabe and his regime were acting in an ever more remorseless and blatant manner.

The persecution of the MDC continued relentlessly. Its supporters, security guards, and even those in the act of addressing rallies, were beaten, raped and murdered by those who knew they were beyond the law. Meanwhile, by torturing men, women and children, Mugabe's henchmen obtained the names and addresses of other MDC activists, whom they could then also persecute. The courage of MDC members shone through like a beacon in a dark world, but as the months and years went by, the number willing to risk their lives – and those of their friends and families – by attending Tsvangirai's rallies, dwindled from the thousands to just a few dozen. Tsvangirai told the simple truth:

> There is violence everywhere, absolutely everywhere. We have no access to the media, we cannot campaign, we are being harassed all the time. How can there be free and fair elections?

Demonstrators with Zanu-PF posters.

MDC supporters march in December 2007.

With much of Zimbabwe, especially the rural areas, held in the grip of terror, MDC leader Tsvangirai was virtually confined to Harare. His rallies were held in secret – as those who attended them knew that they would be hunted down by ZANU-PF mobs. In fact, anyone who did not wear a ZANU-PF T-shirt, or carry a ZANU-PF Party card, was in grave danger.

Said Mugabe:

> If ZANU-PF loses, we will not accept the result. We fought and died for the country and you cannot expect us to hand the country on a silver plate to some new party backed by the white man.[2]

If this is so why did he (and does, at the time of writing) bother to hold elections at all? The answer in part, as will be confirmed time and time again, was that this presented Mugabe with the ideal chance to identify his opponents, whom he could then persecute.

In an ideal world, Mugabe would like to see no opposition whatsoever, with everyone in the country voting for ZANU-PF. However, he goes through the charade of holding elections because, having 'won', he can then convince himself – if no one else – that he has been democratically elected by his people, and that he therefore has their confidence. Also, from what is known of Mugabe's character, it probably gives him enormous pleasure, time and time again, to raise the opposition's hopes before trampling them ruthlessly underfoot. More sinisterly, however, the holding of an election gives him the ideal opportunity to flush his opponents out into the open; to have his henchmen observe them; to see which way they vote and then, if they fail to vote for him, beat, torture, starve and murder them.

The final result, announced on 27 June 2000, was that ZANU-PF had gained 62 seats; the MDC, 57; Independents, 1. However, Mugabe had left nothing to chance, because, even before the election had begun, he had awarded ZANU-PF an extra 30 seats. His Party, therefore, emerged with 92 parliamentary seats (there being 150 in all), sufficient to give him a handsome majority.

The elections had been monitored by a 190-strong observer group from the European Union, headed by Pierre Schori, a former Swedish cabinet minister. Schori observed 'high levels of violence, intimidation and coercion [that had] marred the election campaign', so that they could not be described as 'free and fair'. On 25 October, the MDC demanded Mugabe's impeachment and his removal from office for, 'gross misconduct' and for 'wilful violation of the Constitution'. Needless to say, they were baying at the moon.

The *Daily News,* Zimbabwe's only independent newspaper, had long been a thorn in Mugabe's side, and it was becoming increasingly outspoken. 'Impeach Mugabe!' was a front-page headline, and ZANU-PF was accused of 'betraying our true heroes'. The newspaper also rejoiced when President Kabila of the Congo – one of Mugabe's few remaining allies (for whom 11,000 Zimbabwean troops were currently fighting) – was assassinated. Retribution came in the early hours of 28 January 2001, when its printing press was destroyed in a shattering explosion, believed to have been caused by several anti-tank mines attached to a detonator. However, The *Daily News* obtained another printing press and did not miss printing a single issue from that point forward, until it was finally closed down in September 2003.

It was now time for Mugabe to remove one of the last remnants of electoral opposition. In future elections, anyone wishing to register to vote had to produce title deeds, rental agreements or utility bills for their properties as proof of residence. This meant that hundreds of thousands of impoverished urban MDC supporters – Ndebele and Shona alike – living in shacks in the townships would be disenfranchised. In the rural areas, anyone wishing to vote had to first obtain the personal approval of their village's headman; all of whom were in the pay of the government.

In February 2001, political spokesman Jonathan Moyo, Head of Government Propaganda, demanded that Joe Winter, a BBC reporter, leave the Country within 24 hours, and he sent a mob to Winter's house to reinforce the message. On 30 June, Britain's *Daily Telegraph* reporter David Blair was expelled from Zimbabwe. On 30 November, Mugabe's 'Media and Information Commission' was empowered to prevent journalists from working and to close down newspapers. The alleged murder of a war veteran in Bulawayo on 5 November gave Mugabe the excuse to burn down the MDC's regional headquarters.

Mugabe, for all his cunning and subterfuge, could not prevent the truth from coming out. Sickening pictures of MDU supporters being viciously beaten prior to the presidential elections of March 2002 appeared on television screens throughout the world. Everyone now knew that grievous injuries had been inflicted on those who failed to support ZANU-PF, that hundreds of MDU polling agents had been abducted or intimidated, and that the identity cards of MDU supporters had been stolen in order to prevent them voting. In the words of Welshman Ncube, Secretary-General of the MDC:

> Many of our election agents are missing, and hundreds of people have fled from all over Mashonaland West Province. It is absolutely appalling.

> It appears there is a systematic hunting-down of people who voted for or helped the MDC during the elections.[3]

Although the Mashonaland West voters referred to above would have included some Ndebele, they would have consisted mainly of Shona people – members of Mugabe's own ethnic group. Even this cut no ice with him. All that mattered was that as his political opponents, they must be eliminated. Other voters were simply prohibited from voting, including former Prime Minister Sir Garfield Todd, then aged 93.[4]

In the Presidential Election of March 2002, Mugabe defeated Tsvangirai by 434,000 votes. When a cross-check is made of Zimbabwe's electoral role against its census records, between 1.5 million and 1.9 million people appear to have voted who did not actually exist.

This time, it was the Commonwealth Observer Group who reported on the presidential election, and it was the same old story. They observed that, 'a high level of politically motivated violence and intimidation' had been perpetrated by both sides, mainly by ZANU-PF, and specifically by its paramilitary youth wing. The conclusion was that 'Conditions in Zimbabwe did not adequately allow for a free expression of will by the electors.'

In March 2002, two days after he had been returned to power once more, Mugabe introduced the Access to Information and Protection of Privacy Act. In future, any journalist wishing to work in Zimbabwe must first obtain the approval of a government commission headed by Jonathan Moyo.[5]

On 4 November 2002, Sydney Masamvu, Political Editor of Zimbabwe's *Financial Gazette,* reported on the recent by-election at Insiza in Matabeleland. In the normal course of events, it would have been impossible for the MDC to be defeated in this, their heartland. However, ZANU-PF secured victory (by 12,115 votes to the MDC'S 5,102) but only by 'violence, intimidation and the politicisation of food aid'. The children of MDC supporters in particular had been prevented from receiving food donated by the United Nations World Food Programme – something that 'defenceless and starving rural voters' were unable to withstand. MDC food aid was being held up at Beitbridge on the border with South Africa several months after it had arrived. By then, the number of political murders for 2002 had risen to 54 – more than for the whole of 2001.[6]

On 6 January 2003, it was announced that governors for the cities of Harare and Bulawayo would in future be appointed by Mugabe, rather than be elected as hitherto. This would bring them into line with other

Displaced children living on the streets of Harare.

towns and provinces, whose governors had already been appointed by Mugabe (and who were, naturally, all members of ZANU-PF).[7]

On 12 January, Peter Oborne of *The Spectator* described a recent visit he had made to Zimbabwe: he had entered the country posing as a golfer, but in reality was on a fact-finding mission. Oborne travelled widely, making secret films and recordings. He discovered an all too familiar situation. Maize (from South Africa), was being transported by lorries under state monopoly control to the mills to be ground into 'mealie' meal. ZANU-PF controlled the distribution of the mealie meal, which was for the consumption of its supporters only. In other words, Mugabe's party was now using food as a political weapon. Five members of the United Kingdom's House of Lords expressed grave concern about this, stating that although food aid was reaching Zimbabwe, it was being distributed on a political basis, and only to those who could produce a ZANU-PF party card. Their Lordships urged that observers be put in place as soon as possible to ensure that starving people received the food aid that was intended for them, no matter what political views they held.[8]

On 5 February 2003, Tsvangirai, together with MDC Secretary Welshman Ncube and MP Renson Gasela, were put on trial in Harare, charged under the Law and Order (Maintenance) Act. Tsvangirai was accused of attempting to assassinate Mugabe in the run up to the March

All blasted? All wasted?

Tsvangirai with head wound, March 2007.

2002 Presidential Elections, and charged with treason. This was on the basis of a videotape in which he had, allegedly, referred to Mugabe as someone who needed to be 'eliminated'. In his defence, Tsvangirai claimed that he had been framed, and that the word 'elimination' referred to the ballot box.[9] Why was the trial held at this particular time, when the alleged offence had taken place a year previously? Undoubtedly, to prevent Tsvangirai and his colleagues from participating in the forthcoming presidential elections, which were due to be held in two months time. (In the event, Tsvangirai and his colleagues were acquitted.)

In November 2005, following a rift in the MDC, Tsvangirai continued to lead its (mainly Shona) supporters in Harare, whilst Welshman Ncube lead its (mainly Ndbele) supporters in Matabeleland.

The iron grip of Mugabe's totalitarianism even enveloped Zimbabwe's Anglican Church. The Anglican Bishop of Harare, Nolbert Kunonga, was in the habit of heaping unstinting praise on Mugabe. Furthermore, any priest of his who dared to speak out against Mugabe found himself transferred to a remote parish and intimidated. The result was that between 2003 and 2005, more than thirty Anglican priests from Harare left the country. For his pains, Kunonga was rewarded with the gift of St Marnocks Farm, which was seized from its former white owner Marcus Hale.[10]

A rally and prayer meeting, held on 11 March 2007 by Tsvangirai on the outskirts of Harare, was disrupted by Mugabe's police, who made multiple arrests and administered many beatings. MDC member Gift Tandare was shot dead. Tsvangirai himself suffered a broken hand, multiple bruises, major internal bleeding, and had his head banged repeatedly against a wall. Although a brain scan revealed that there was no fracture of Tsvangirai's skull, he nevertheless required a transfusion of two units of blood, and the deep gash in his head required eight stitches.

Another person to be severely injured was Sekai Holland, a 64-year-old grandmother, who had been married for 40 years to Australian national Jim Holland. During Ian Smith's period of white minority rule, Sekai had lived in exile in Australia, where she had campaigned against racism, injustice, and apartheid. In 1980, she returned to the newly-born Zimbabwe, full of hope and joy, and devoted herself to building a multiracial democracy. She was now the MDC's Secretary for Party Development. For having participated in Tsvangirai's peaceful rally, Sekai was assaulted by a female police officer, who stamped repeatedly on her chest and back, and by several policemen, who clubbed her – especially about the head and neck – with batons. The result was fractures to both arms, an ankle, and several ribs, with severe, generalised bruising. Sekai was clearly targeted for being a supporter of the opposition MDC Party. However, there was another reason why she had incurred the wrath of the Mugabe regime, as her fellow MDC supporter Grace Kwinje – who was also beaten – explained: 'They tortured her because she is married to a White.'[11]

Mugabe was unrepentant:

> Tsvangirai deserved his beating up by police because he was not allowed to attend a banned rally. The police have the right, the right to bash them. They will get arrested and bashed by the police.[12]

Edward Chikomba, who is believed to have courageously smuggled video footage out of the country that showed the injuries sustained by Tsvangirai, was subsequently abducted from his home on the outskirts of Harare and murdered.[13]

As night follows day, Mugabe accused others of crimes for which he was responsible:

> It's the West as usual. When they criticise the government [for] trying to prevent violence and punish the perpetrators of that violence, we take the position that they can go hang.[14]

Time for some R&R; Mugabe flew off to join his wife Grace, who was holidaying in Thailand.

June 2007 found Mugabe's government drafting laws permitting it to monitor telephone calls and e-mails.

11

Mugabe's Loathing of the White Farmers

In the years following independence in 1980, land ownership became the subject of bitter conflict and controversy. In order to understand Mugabe's resentment of, and consequent hostility to, Zimbabwe's white farmers, one must know how they came into possession of their vast lands in the first place.

From at least 5,000 BC, the land which became Zimbabwe was inhabited by the Bushmen. Caves were their preferred habitat, but they also lived in primitive huts made of branches. Their skill as trackers was legendary.

The Matopos, situated in Matabeleland to the south of Bulawayo, encompasses a great range of granite hills, extending over 1,250 square miles and topped by enormous boulders and groups of balancing rocks, overlooking wooded valleys. There are many caves here in which the Bushmen have left their legacy, in the form of Rock Art, which dates from about the 1st millennium AD, and which reached its peak in Matabeleland in the 16th century and 17th century.[1] The rock art indicates they were hunters and that they probably lived a nomadic lifestyle.

Their fate was decided by a people who came originally from the Niger/Congo region of Central Africa, known as the 'Bantu'. They shared a common language (of which there are over 200 sub-groups), and had learned to cultivate crops and to forge tools from metals. From the 17th century to the 19th century, the Bantu extended their sphere of influence by colonising the whole of Central and southern Africa.[2] On the arrival of the Bantu, the Bushmen were simply murdered or driven into the country's western deserts. (There are now no Bushmen remaining in Zimbabwe, and fewer than 2,000 in South West Africa.)

Those Bantu who colonised what is now Zimbabwe, are collectively called the Mashona (or Shona), which consists of sub-groups including Zezuru, Karanga, Tonga-Korekore, Manica, and Ndau.

In the year 1838, the Bantu were themselves invaded. The Zulus, who were members of the same Bantu ethnic group as the Shona, colonised the region of south-eastern Africa, subsequently known as Natal. In about 1824, Moselekatse, a commander in the Zulu army, omitted to send tribute (obligatory payment) to Tshaka, the Zulu king, following a successful raiding expedition. When Tshaka sent a punitive expedition to destroy him, Moselekatse fled across the Drakensberg Mountains, and began to lay waste to the land later known as the Orange Free State and the Transvaal. Early in 1838, after battles with both Boers and Zulus, Moselekatse was once again forced to flee, this time northwards across the Limpopo river. He and his people duly settled near the Bembesi river, in what later became Southern Rhodesia.

According to Mrs Phoebe Taylor of the Kuruman Mission Station in Bechuanaland, the Shona inhabitants of that region, instead of meekly submitting to Moselekatse, offered him some resistance.

> The bow and arrow was the principal weapon used by the Mashonas [Shona], but they also had some muzzle-loading rifles traded from us [the British]. Arrows and spears were all poisoned, and many of the Matabele [Moselekatse's warriors] who were hit probably died later on.[3]

Nonetheless, the Shona were either murdered, enslaved, or driven into the hills. Moselekatse now established his capital at Inyati, and called his newly won territory Matabeleland. His followers became known as the Matabele (or Ndebele, meaning 'those who disappear' – that is, are able to blend easily into the bush.)

Moselekatse, who became known as the first King of the Matabele, died in 1868. He was succeeded by his son Lobengula, who proceeded from his capital Gubulawayo, (later Bulawayo) to establish his sway over a wide area, almost completely subduing the local Mashona in the process. So when the white man arrived in 1890, the country was occupied primarily by these two ethnic groups, the Shona and the Ndebele.

Although the first white settlers to establish themselves in the country were the missionaries (in the year 1859) it was Cecil John Rhodes who was primarily responsible for the continuing and increasing presence of whites in the land.

Rhodes was born at Bishop's Stortford in Hertfordshire, England on 5 July 1853. Suffering from tuberculosis, he was sent at the age of 17 to

& 2 Wildlife of the Wankie Game Reserve. The animals of Zimbabwe suffer alongside the ꞉eople, with preservation efforts in disarray.

3 Rock art in the caves of the Matopos Hills.

4 On the farm in 1950s Southern Rhodesia; preparing for lessons.

Strip road from Gwelo to Selukwe.

Employees of Glengarry School for Whites, 1950s.

7 & 8 Labour MP Kate Hoey is chairman of the all-party group on Zimbabwe in Westminster. She has visited the country several times on fact-finding missions, undercover i recent years. 'Zimbabwe has gone from the bread-basket of Africa to a failed state under an increasingly brutal dictator. This is a modern tragedy.'

9 The bread-basket of Africa; empty shelves in a Harare supermarket.

10 Mugabe and wife Grace. Mugabe wears his usual campaigning 'man-of-the-people' baseball cap.

11 & 12 Families are evicted, prior to their homes being demolished in Operation Murambatsvina.

3 Anti-riot police stand guard after a family home is destroyed during Operation Murambatsvina.

Morgan Tsvangirai addressing a rally.

15 Mugabe relaxed at an official function.

16 A bulldozer destroys a home in a suburb of Harare.

17 Bulldozed then burned.

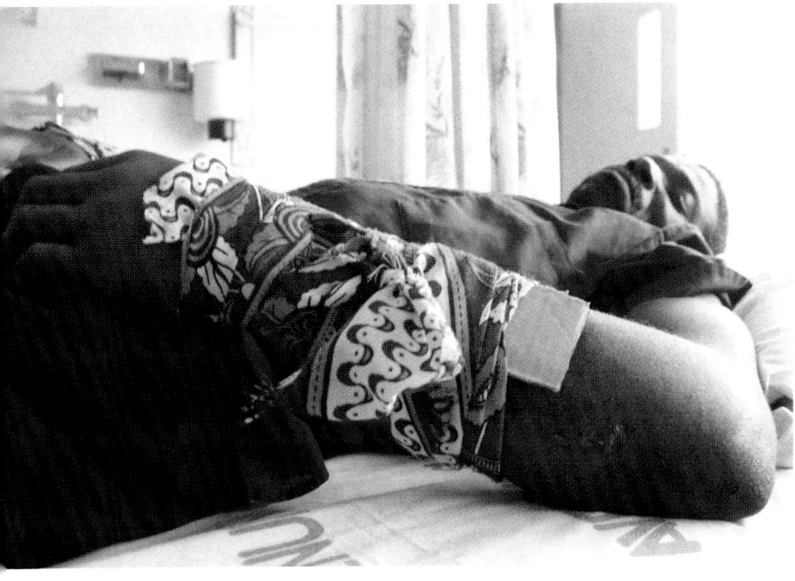

18 4 April 2008. A man from Mashonaland lies in a hospital bed in Harare after being beaten.

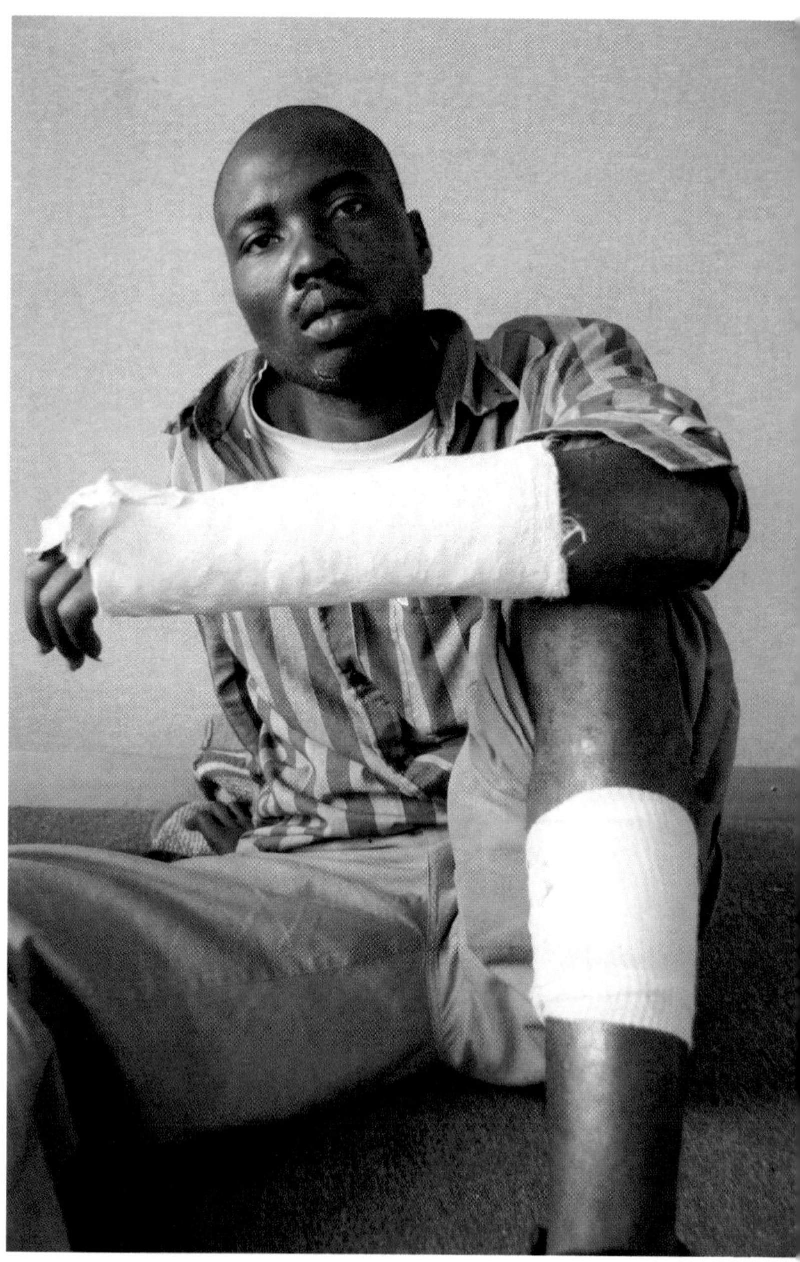

19 3 May 2008. A man from Masvingo Province who took refuge at the MDC's headquarters in Harare shows the results of beatings.

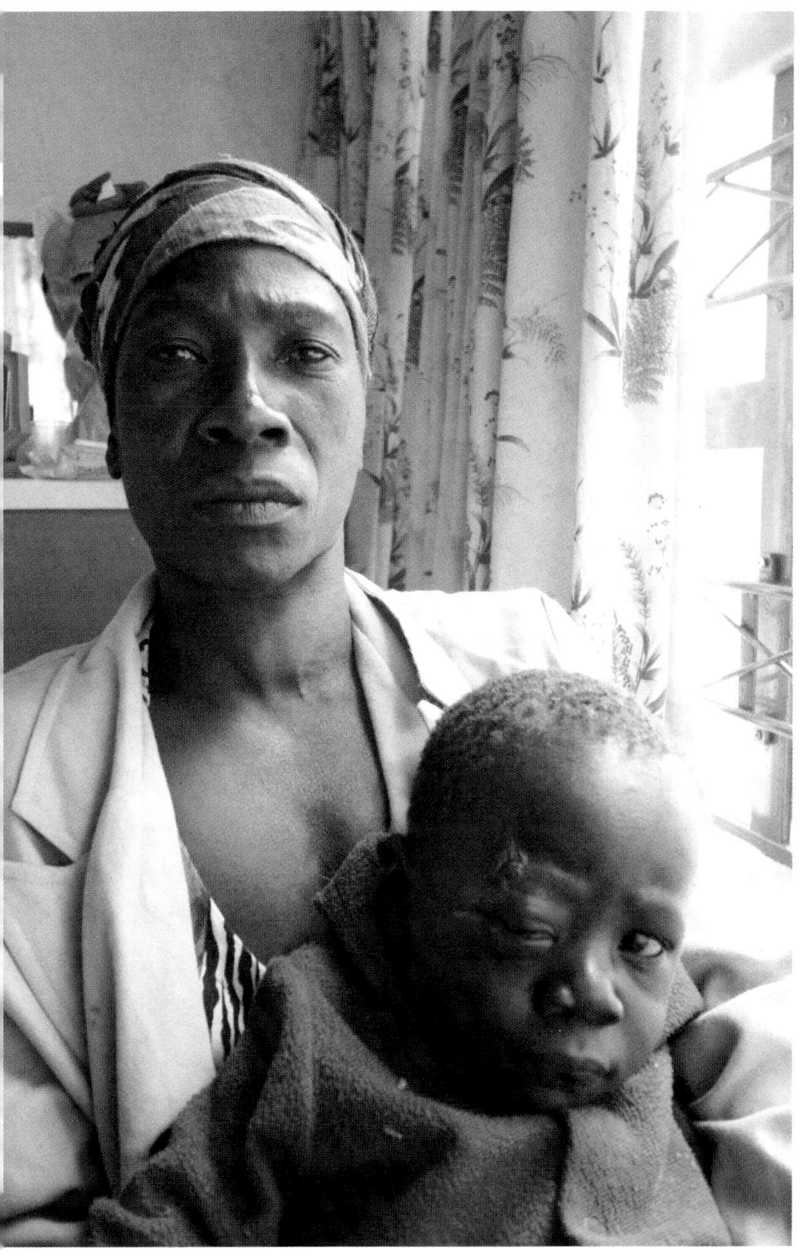

20 9 May 2008. Samson Chemerani, aged three, with his mother from central Mashonaland, receives medical care at a clinic in Harare. He was caught in crossfire as his parents' huts were torched by ZANU-PF supporters.

21 'From him that hath not shall be taken away even that which he hath.' (Matthew 25:29). Such homes live in fear.

-29 This page and overleaf: surveying the wreckage and picking up the pieces.

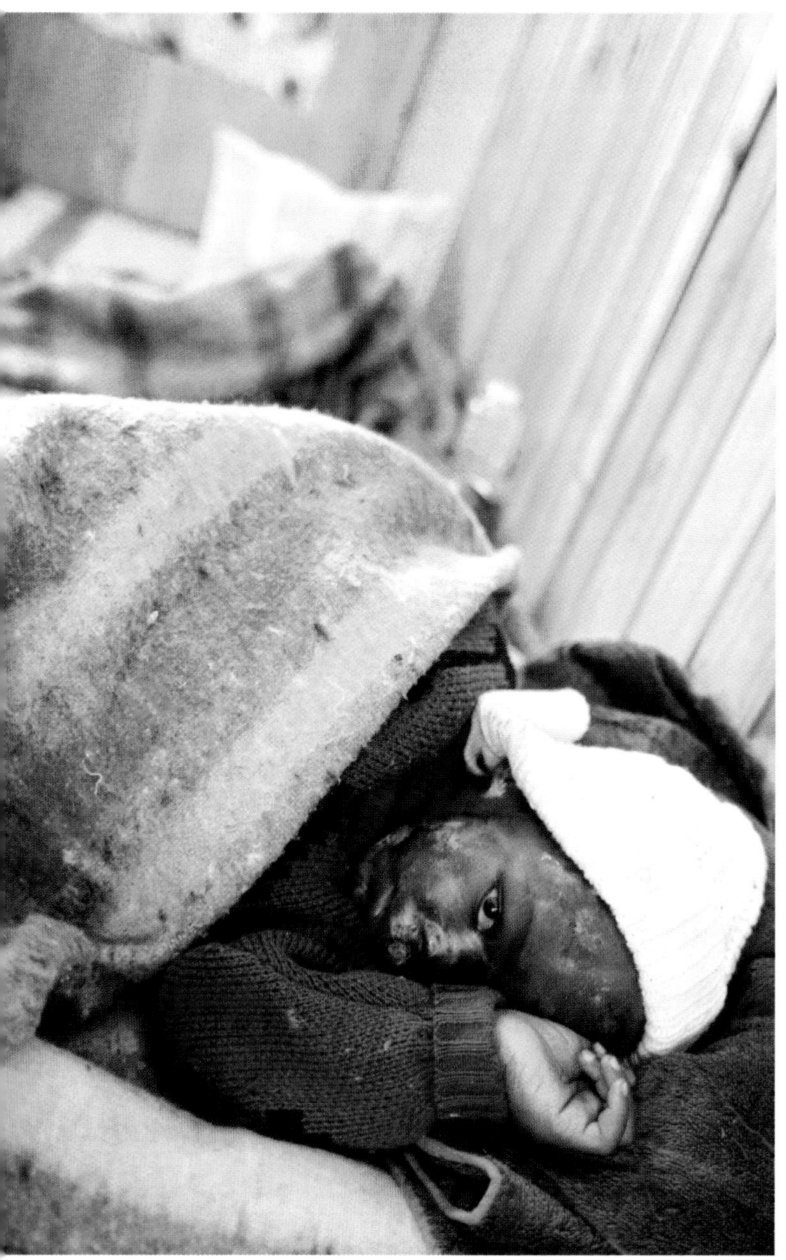

The handmaiden of malnutrition and neglect is disease.

31 Mugabe and wife Grace celebrate.

32 Remains of the Batsirai Children's Centre at Hatfield Extension, Harare, formerly home to more than 100 orphans, many of whom were suffering from HIV and AIDS.

3 Saving what can be saved, Hatfield Extension, 30 May, 2005.

4 All that's left, Killarney, Bulawayo.

35 The intimidation of the opposition in Zimbabwe that the world is aware of and condemns in 2008 is nothing new. A Movement for Democratic Change (MDC) supporter sits in protest, surrounded by riot police, outside the Harare High Court before the arrival of party President Morgan Tsvangirai, October 15, 2004. Tsvangirai was in cour for judgement in a treason trial for an alleged conspiracy to assassinate Mugabe ahead of the Presidential Election in 2002. Mugabe's regime was not such big news back then. Perhaps if it had been, the escalation of terror in the intervening years could have been averted. (Howard Burditt/Reuters/Corbis)

Ready to start over.

The beginnings of a new house, perhaps a home.

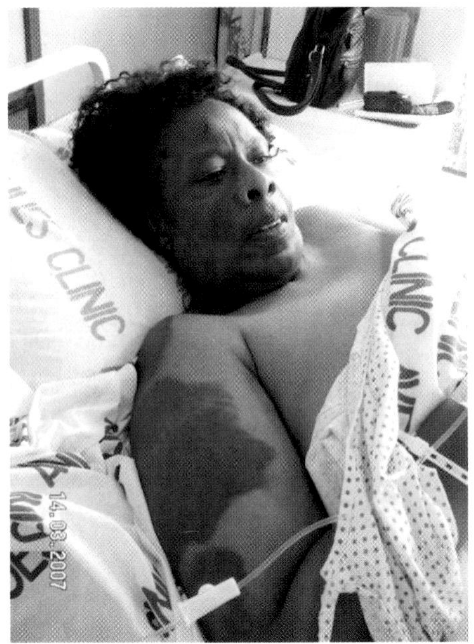

38 Sekai Holland of the MDC, bea

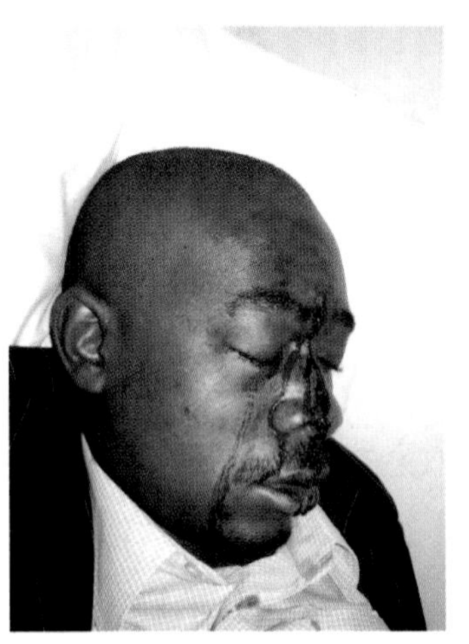

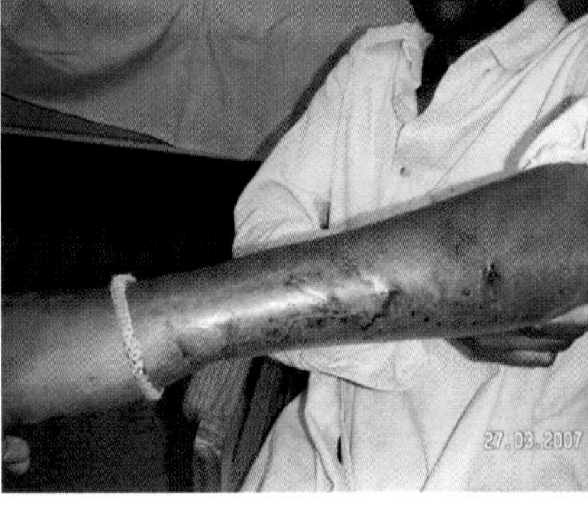

39 & *40* Victims of brutality.

The new homeless play cards by firelight.

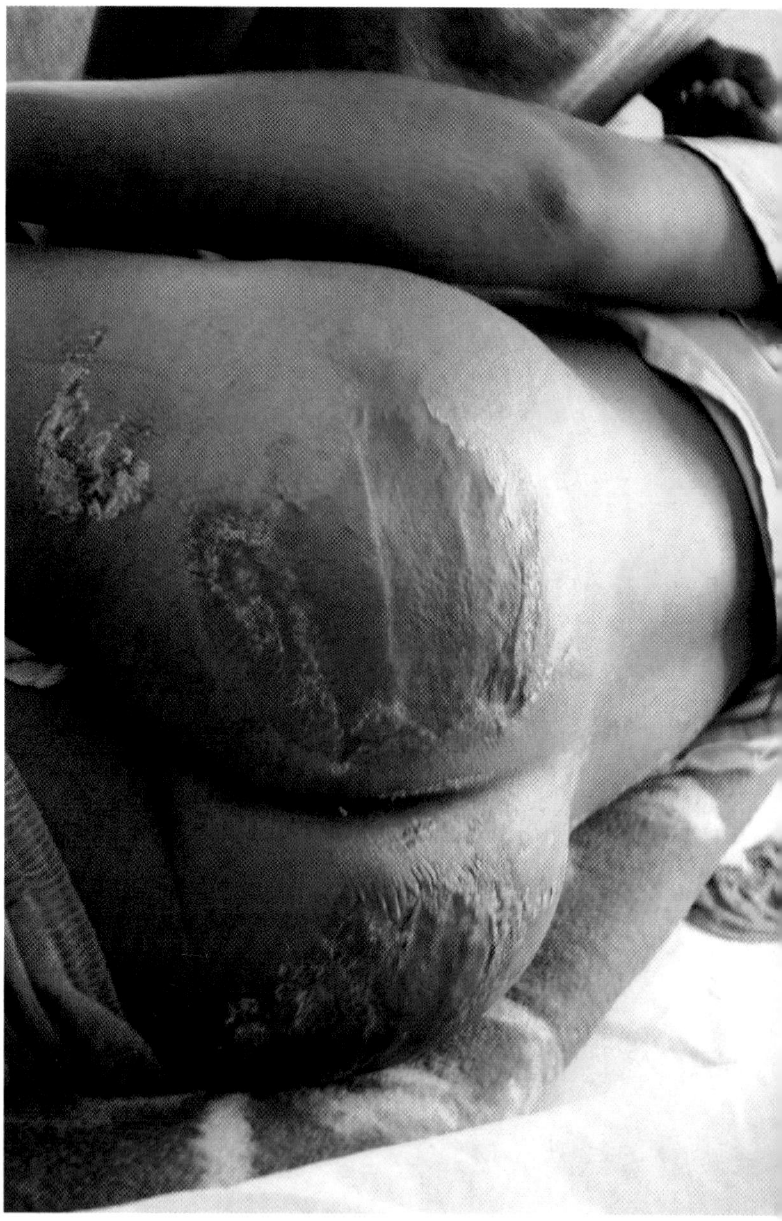

42 & 43 Savage beatings meted out to those deemed not to support the ruling regime, designed not only to injure and scar but also to humiliate. Should we publish such pictures? The author and publishers have considered this question long and hard. People risked their lives to to take them. These men are teachers.

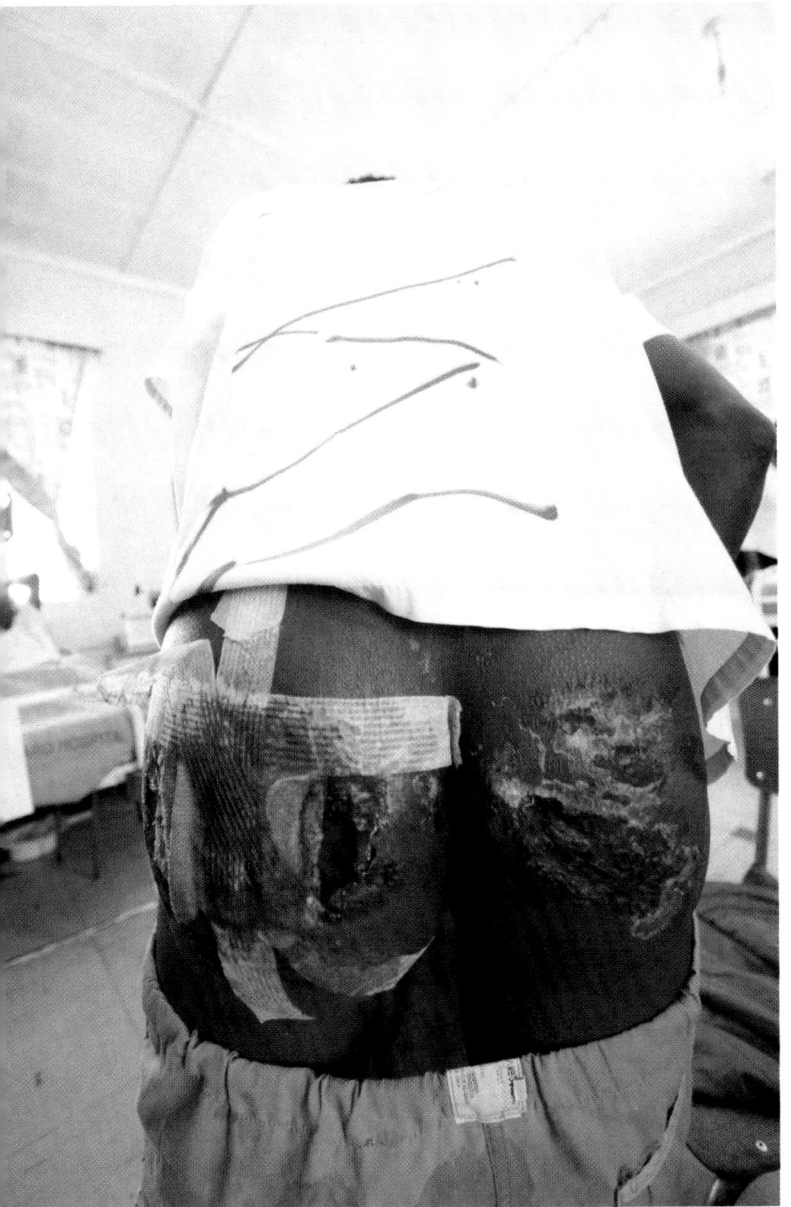

44 Hope for the future? MDC slogans, Harare.

the British Crown Colony of Natal (where his brother was already an established farmer) in the hope that the clean air would improve his health. It did, and when diamonds were discovered at Kimberley in the Orange Free State, Rhodes moved there and prospered by setting up in business selling excavating equipment and water pumps to the newly-opened mines. In 1880 he founded the De Beers Diamond Mining Company — and the rest really is history. Rhodes was active in politics, and in 1884 was appointed to the Cabinet of the Cape Colony and served as its Treasurer. When gold was discovered on the 'Rand' (Witwatersrand – an area south of Johannesburg in the Transvaal), Rhodes invested in these fields, and in 1887, established the Goldfields of South Africa Company.

In 1888, the ever ambitious Rhodes sent Charles Rudd, his business partner at Kimberley and two others northwards to meet with the Matabele King, Lobengula. Their purpose was to secure rights to the mineral deposits in his territory, which they knew of from previous exploration. Rudd offered Lobengula 1,000 rifles, 10,000 bullets, a steamboat with guns for use on the Zambesi river, and £1,200 a year for himself and his heirs, in return for which the latter signed away the mineral rights to his 'kingdom, principalities and dominions'. The signed document, known as the 'Rudd Concession', was at once sent to Rhodes in South Africa. He presented it to the British Government which, a year later, granted a royal charter for his newly created British South Africa Company (BSAC).

Rhodes' problems were not quite over, because prior to the arrival if his emissary Rudd, the German Edward Lippert had visited Lobengula and obtained from the King mineral concessions of considerable value in Matabeleland. Rhodes was therefore obliged to negotiate with Lippert in order to be able to exploit his own mining interests in that region. This resulted in 1889 in the signing of the 'Lippert Concession', which allowed would-be British settlers to acquire land rights from the indigenous people. (In practice, the BSAC bought concessions from the British Crown and then sold them to the settlers; the revenue accruing to the Crown. The black owners of the land received nothing.)

Rhodes now contracted 23-year-old Major Frank Johnson, formerly of the Bechuanaland Border Police, to organise a pioneer column which would occupy Mashonaland. This would consist of 200 hired adventurers – none of them over the age of 25 – together with 117 waggons, to be guided by the famous elephant hunter Frederick Courteney Selous. As the BSAC was unable to afford the expense of maintaining a paid occupation force, Jameson, the BSAC's administrator, agreed that the

Cecil Rhodes' grave, Matopos.

prospective settlers should each receive a farm, 'of 3,000 morgen' (about 6,300 acres) for volunteering to join the expedition, together with twenty gold claims.[4] A document signed to this effect by Jameson, became known as the 'Victorian Agreement'.

Those who followed in the footsteps of the pioneers were treated even more generously, and Jameson awarded vast tracts of land to wealthy individuals and syndicates, on condition that they spend agreed sums of money on the development of their property. Rhodes's aides were also extremely well rewarded. Major Sir John Willoughby, the Pioneer Column's second in command, was awarded 600,000 acres, after promising to spend £50,000 on their development.[5] (His Consolidated Company eventually owned 1.3 million acres.) Rhodes's surveyor-general, on taking up his post, was awarded 640,000 acres. The missionaries also benefited – acquiring almost one third of a million acres. This meant that within ten years, a total of about 16 million acres – one sixth of the land area of Southern Rhodesia – had been appropriated by whites.

From July 1893 to January 1894, British forces were at war with the Matabele. In March 1896, the Matabele rose up once more against the British and were finally subdued in October 1897. The victorious whites now established a Legislative Assembly, Rhodes promising that eventually, the country would be granted self-government. Meanwhile, the Native Reserves Order in Council of 1898 created areas designated specifically for blacks only, which were of only mediocre quality, the whites having appropriated the most fertile portions for themselves. This had an added advantage for the whites, in that the blacks, being unable to make a satisfactory living at home, were forced to look outside their reserves for jobs, which they found on white-owned farms and in white-owned businesses.

Although the system of apartheid is regarded as a modern phenomenon, it had its roots in an act of parliament introduced by Cecil Rhodes in 1894, and known as The Native Reserves Order in Council. The first Native Reserve was created by Rhodes at Glen Grey in a region between the Cape Colony and Natal, known as Kaffraria (part of which was annexed by the Cape Colony in 1885). 'My idea,' said Rhodes, 'is that the natives should be kept in these native reserves and not mixed with white men at all.'[6] Rhodes can, therefore, be justifiably described as being the first architect of apartheid.

Within the reserve, each black man received an 8-acre allotment on which he was expected to produce enough food to provide for himself and his family. As this was virtually impossible, he was forced to sell his labour outside the reserve to a white farmer or industrialist. Should he fail to do so within a 12-month period, he would be liable to pay a 'labour tax' in addition to the 'hut tax' payable by every family.[7] Blacks had no voting rights outside the reserve, but were permitted to elect 'native councillors' within it.[8] Finally, they were forbidden to sell their land, even if they so wished.

Rhodes told the Members of Parliament 'The whole of the North will sometime or other come under this bill if [it is] passed in the House ... This is a native bill for Africa.' In other words, this was to be the blueprint for the establishment of native reserves throughout the whole of British-ruled southern and Central Africa.[9]

By the year 1914 (when the total population of blacks in Southern Rhodesia was 836,000, and of whites 28,000) the land had been apportioned (in millions of acres) as follows:

British South Africa Company (BSAC)	48
Blacks (in designated native reserves)	24
Individual white settlers	13
Private companies	9[10]

In practical terms, this meant that 3 per cent of the population, the whites, were in possession of 75 per cent of the land. And the land assigned to the blacks was of inferior quality.

In 1918, the Judicial Committee of the Privy Council in London issued a ruling that the land of Southern Rhodesia was owned by the Crown, and not by the BSAC. In 1923, which was the year that the BSAC's Charter expired, a referendum was held in which the whites of Southern Rhodesia voted for domestic self-government. A Westminster-style parliamentary system was created and Bulawayo lawyer Charles Coghlan became Southern Rhodesia's first Prime Minister. Britain retained a continuing role in determining policy apropos the blacks. Only British subjects were entitled to vote.

The Land Apportionment Act of 1930 formalised the division of land between blacks and whites (the black population having now grown to 1.1 million, and the white to 50,000) as follows (in millions of acres):

Whites	49
Blacks (in designated native reserves)	29
Unassigned, or devoted to forests or national parks	9
Native Purchase Areas (available for purchase by black farmers)	8[11]

The Act also stipulated that no black was entitled to own land in a white area. When Sir Godfrey Huggins became Prime Minister in 1933, he summarised the position thus:

> The Europeans in this country can be likened to an island in a sea of black, with the artisan and the tradesman forming the shores and the professional classes the highlands in the centre. Is the native to be allowed to erode the shores and gradually attack the highlands?

This, then, was the background to land ownership in Southern Rhodesia. At the Lancaster House Conference in 1979, it was agreed that for the first ten years following independence there would be no compulsory acquisition of land by the government, and that a willing seller/willing buyer principle would apply.

In March 1981, at the instigation of Britain, the Zimbabwean Conference on Reconstruction and Redevelopment (ZIMCORD) was convened at Salisbury, at which in excess of £636 million of aid was pledged to Zimbabwe (mainly by Britain, West Germany, and the USA.) This included the provision of finance for the Land Reform Programme.

Someone who had first-hand experience of a colony becoming independent was President Samora Machel of Mozambique. Although Machel had preached racial tolerance prior to Mozambique's independence in July 1975, virtually the entire Portuguese population of

250,000 had fled the country. As a result, Mozambique was now desperately short not only of agriculturalists, but also of engineers, doctors and veterinary surgeons (the Portuguese having failed to train any blacks for such professions). The vacuum left by the white exodus quickly became apparent. Mozambique's new collective state farms – created along Marxist lines – lacked not only machinery, but also those with the expertise to manage them. The result was that for the first time, Mozambique was forced to import its basic foodstuffs and by 1979 its balance of payments deficit was US$230 million. The national chain of 'people's shops', established by Machel, failed dismally, partly because of the lack of marketing expertise of their owners. Machel had the humility to admit what the problem was and also indicated how he would attempt to rectify it.

> The state will create the conditions to support private traders, farmers and industrialists. Private activity has an important role to play in straightening out the country.

On 9 January 1980, Machel, at Mugabe's invitation, addressed Mugabe's Central Committee in Maputo. Urging moderation and pragmatism to the committee's hard-line Marxists, he drew a clear distinction between the 'lackadaisical, corrupt and cruel' Portuguese colonists and the Rhodesian whites who, he said, had much to offer the new country.[12] He then gave a stark warning to Mugabe: 'You will face ruin if you force the whites there into precipitate flight.'

Mugabe may be forgiven for feeling that Zimbabwe's white farmers had profited at the expense of the blacks. However, it was a fact of life that when he came to power in 1980, the white-owned farms provided practically all of the nation's food, including maize, which was the staple diet of the blacks. Zimbabwe, known in those days as the 'bread basket of Africa', was a net exporter of food, which made a vital contribution to the country's balance of payments.

Anyone with a modicum of common sense would have heeded Machel's wise words. And Mugabe, with a degree in economics, ought to have been alive to the economic realities. He should also have known that farming is a highly skilled business, and that a farm does not simply appear, but has to be built up with hard work over many years. In 1980 Mugabe must have realised that only by working with the white farmers did he have any hope of continuing to feed his people. And yet, he gradually appropriated white farms for his henchmen, who sat idly by as the weeds grew, the machinery rusted, and the irrigation systems fell into disrepair. He continued with this policy until virtually all the white farms had been requisitioned and food production had dropped to such a low level that the country was forced to depend on handouts from various aid organisations.

At the very beginning of the land appropriation exercise, Mugabe would have liked nothing more than for the white farmers to have donated their best farms voluntarily to his ZANU-PF Party and the remainder to the war veterans, together with all machinery and possessions, down to the last Zimbabwean dollar; then for them all to leave the country. When they did not, they immediately became his enemies: they had to be stripped of their assets, rendered homeless and reduced to beggary. As had been demonstrated on countless previous occasions, vindictiveness was part of Mugabe's make up.

12

Farm Appropriation: Famine

At the beginning of the 1980s, Zimbabwe's economy was booming; the most important economic activity – and the one upon which the livelihoods of four-fifths of the population depended — being agriculture. At independence in 1980, 39 per cent of the land was owned by 6,000 white farmers, who employed 300,000 black workers. The 8,000 black farmers owned only 4 per cent of the land.

In 1981, the land supported five million cattle, 386,000 sheep, 1,335,000 goats and 146,000 pigs. Two million tons of maize was produced per annum – more than double the country's requirements, and the surplus was exported. In 1981–82, 89 million kilograms of tobacco was produced, 96 per cent of which was exported.[1]

The Land Acquisition Act of 1985 (which was based on the willing seller/willing buyer principle agreed at Lancaster House,) gave the government first refusal to purchase white farms whenever they happened to come on the market, and to settle them with blacks. However, because whites were either unwilling to sell their land or demanded too high a price for it in the eyes of the government when they did so, only 71,000 out of an intended 162,000 black families had been resettled in the first decade following independence.[2]

The Land Acquisition Act of 1992 was designed to accelerate the process of land redistribution, by removing the willing seller/willing buyer principle and empowering the government to purchase land compulsorily. Compensation was to be paid to the white farmer, who was given the right of legal appeal should he not agree that the price set was reasonable. The land targeted for acquisition in this Act was derelict land; under-utilised land; land owned by absentee landlords; land belonging to farmers with more than one farm, or with overly large farms; and land adjacent to communal areas.

In July 1992, the government went beyond the confines of the 1992 Act by designating certain white farms, and some owned by blacks, for acquisition that did not fit into any of these categories. In 1993 70 farms were designated, including those belonging to the Reverend Ndabaningi Sithole, ZANU's first leader prior to Mugabe, and James Chikerema, another of Mugabe's political opponents. This was not simply an acquisition of land by Mugabe, it was also a revenge attack on his former political rivals (in this case black), regardless of the fact that they no longer posed any credible threat to him. This was the same behaviour he had exhibited when he had hounded Joshua Nkomo out of the government a decade previously.

When a group of farmers decided to challenge the legality of the 1992 Land Acquisition Act, Mugabe responded angrily: 'We will not brook any decision by any court [to prevent us] from acquiring any land.'[3]

The spectre of corruption and nepotism now raised its ugly head, as many if not most of the acquired farms were donated to members of Mugabe's ZANU-PF Party (including government ministers and officials) and to already wealthy businessmen who supported Mugabe. In reaction to such overt corruption, Britain and the USA ceased to give financial support to the Land Reform Programme.

Adopting some of the principles of Maoist communism, Mugabe established collectives, whereby blacks were settled on land (to which they had no title), where they were expected to grow food for the mutual benefit of themselves and others. What happened in practice was that the settlers were conveyed to their new farms to find that the water pumps which fed the vital irrigation systems and also supplied drinking water had either fallen into disrepair, or had been stolen or vandalised. This, together with an absence of seed, fertiliser, livestock, supervision or financial backing, left them with no alternative but to loot what they could before quietly returning from whence they came. The farms then became derelict.

In 1997, the Government tightened the screw. It drafted a new constitution containing a clause which enabled it to avoid paying any compensation. In September 1998, the International Donors' Conference on Land Reform and Resettlement was held in Harare. Forty-eight countries participated, and pledged technical and financial support for the programme.

In February 2000, the government held a referendum on a proposed new constitution. The government was defeated, but Mugabe amended the existing constitution anyway, to authorise land appropriation without consultation and to make Britain responsible for the cost of farm appropriation.

A period of mob violence now ensued, when Mugabe authorised war veterans to seize farms from their owners by force. Chakwana Mueri, otherwise known as 'Comrade Jesus', of ZANU-PF was particularly active in inciting mobs of drugged and drunken veterans to rampage through white farms in an orgy of looting, burning, beating and destruction; the goal of which was to force the white farmers to sign away the rights to their farms on the spot.

In the June 2000 election (which ZANU-PF won by 62 seats to the MDC's 57), ZANU-PF campaigned on the land issue. 'The end has come. Land will now come to the people' was the Party's message. That November, the Commercial Farmers' Union (CFU) challenged Mugabe's 'fast track' Land Resettlement Programme in the Supreme Court. The case was heard by 68-year-old Chief Justice Anthony Gubbay. He found in the CFU's favour. Mugabe, not for the first time, showed his disdain for the law by appearing on television and declaring: 'Whatever the courts might say on the matter, the land is ours and we will take it.' Gubbay, who had had the temerity to defy Mugabe, was subsequently hounded out of office when his court was invaded by a mob. He agreed in March 2001 to take leave until his official retirement in July.

On 7 September 2001, at a Commonwealth foreign ministers' meeting in Nigeria's capital Abuja, Britain offered the sum of £36 million for land reform, as long as the redistribution was done legally and peacefully and was combined with macroeconomic reforms.[4] Mugabe continued with his own agenda.

The Land Acquisition Act was then amended so that any farmer served with a 'Section 8 Occupation Order' had three months to vacate his farm. Meanwhile, the maize crop yield had fallen by 42 per cent, prompting the Famine Early Warning Network (funded by the US Agency for International Development) to declare that the Country would face famine in early 2002.

At midnight on 23 June 2002, the final Notices of Acquisition, which gave 2,900 of Zimbabwe's remaining 3,500 white farmers notice to cease their operations immediately and vacate their farms by mid-August, came into effect. Those who refused to leave would face up to two years imprisonment.

At the annual opening of Parliament in July 2002, Mugabe hailed the land redistribution scheme as, 'an unparalleled success' and announced

'We were forced to destroy our own homes.'

that almost half of the 5,000 white-owned commercial farms had been transferred to blacks. He either could not see, or would not acknowledge, that as far as food production was concerned it was a disaster.

In September 2002, the Government, not content with confiscating farms, gazetted legislation ordering dispossessed farmers to pay retrenchment money to their former employees. No upper limit was set as to the amount that an employee might seek, even if he or she had worked on a farm for as short a period as one month.

In October 2002, Mugabe openly began to use his police force to impose his will on the white farmers. Now, instead of standing idly by – as they had done for many months, whilst the war veterans had pursued their brutal campaign – the police began to play an active role, arriving on the farms and manhandling their occupants.

In the same month, UN officials confirmed that Mugabe had banned the charities Oxfam and Save the Children from distributing food aid in the country.[5] In November, members of an aid mission that included an employee of the American Embassy in Harare and an official of the United Nations were beaten by Mugabe's war veterans. They were studying how to assist former farm workers who had been displaced by the land seizures and who were surviving on a diet of berries and

A woman watches her home being demolished.

termites. The aid workers' offense was to throw food from their moving vehicle to these farm workers.

In December 2002, the World Food Programme declared that at least 6.7 million Zimbabweans would require emergency food aid in the coming months.[6]

Over the next three years the situation continued to deteriorate. Nonetheless, in August 2005, Mugabe refused to endorse a humanitarian appeal by the United Nations for US$30 million, for food and blankets which were to be donated to 300,000 of those hardest hit by his 'Operation Murambatsvina' ('Operation Drive out Trash') in which Mugabe had destroyed squatter camps around Bulawayo and Victoria Falls the previous May. In a speech to the UN Conference on Food Safety in October 2005, Mugabe said:

> In our fight for freedom and independence, one of the pillars of the struggle was land grievance – land, land, land, which means food, food, food to the people.

The world was not deceived, for by now, everyone had seen images of Zimbabweans queuing for hours for a loaf of bread outside supermarkets where there was nothing on the shelves, and walking around like living skeletons. How utterly cruel and callous Mugabe's words must have seemed to people such as these.

In that year, Zimbabwe's troubles were compounded by a drought when January's rains, so crucial for the irrigation of newly-planted crops, failed to materialise. This was in a country which, according to the International Crisis Group, already had between 4 million and 5 million internal refugees – about one third of the population of 13 million.

In February 2007, the final 400 white farmers were given notice to quit – at least twelve having so far been killed during the Land Appropriation Programme. By September, Zimbabwe was obliged to import about 37,000 tonnes of maize per week.

13

Racism, Homophobia, Genocide

Mugabe's exclusion of ZAPU leader Joshua Nkomo from the Independence Day celebrations of 18 April 1980 and hounding him out of the government was a foretaste of things to come. ZANU's Manifesto for the election of March 1980 declared:

> Zanu wishes to give the fullest assurance to the white community, the Asian and Coloured communities that a ZANU government can never, in principle or in social or government practice, discriminate against them. Racism, whether practised by Whites or Blacks, is an anathema to the humanitarian philosophy of ZANU. It is as primitive a dogma as tribalism or regionalism. Zimbabwe cannot just be a country for Blacks. It is and should remain our country, all of us together.[1]

The words turned to ashes in January 1983, when Mugabe struck at the heart of Nkomo's support when he sent the North Korean-trained 5th Brigade into Matabeleland North to deal with ex-ZIPRA 'dissidents' from Nkomo's former guerrilla army. Even though these dissidents were thought to number only a few hundred, Mugabe began a campaign of ethnic cleansing that he directed against the entire Ndebele people of the region. Rape, beating, torture, burning, and deliberate starvation resulted in the deaths of an estimated 10,000 people.

In 1984, following an upsurge of 'dissident' activity' in Matabeleland South, in which several white farmers were killed, the 5th Brigade was sent there to reprise its previous heinous activities. This time, not only did it attempt to starve the region's entire population of 400,000, it also flung an estimated 8,000 murdered bodies down disused mine shafts, only to have them float to the surface again when the rains came. In 1988, Mugabe pre-empted any possible repercussions by declaring an amnesty for the soldiers of the infamous 5th Brigade, rendering them immune from prosecution.

In January 1998, there were food riots in the black townships of Harare – a stronghold of MDC support – even though the population there was mainly Shona. Instead of addressing the problem, Mugabe deployed the army. Several people were killed and hundreds more injured.

On 10 March 2000, Mugabe made a speech in which he declared, 'We want the whites to learn that the land belongs to the Zimbabweans.' Clearly, Mugabe did not regard the whites as legitimate citizens of the country. In an interview in June 2000 with David Dimbleby of the BBC, Mugabe demonstrated once again that he was still playing his double game:

> We ourselves should not ever … as a government, as a Party, as individuals within the Party, be seen to be acting in a racist way, blacks against whites, we refuse to do that. The whites wouldn't be here if I was like that … we can't do things like that.[2]

Contrast this with what he told the ZANU-PF Congress in December 2000:

> This country is our country and this land is our land … They think because they are white they have a divine right to our resources. Not here. The white man is not indigenous to Africa. Africa is for Africans. Zimbabwe is for Zimbabweans.[3]

On 16 October 2000, riots broke out again in the black townships of Harare, following a 34 per cent increase in the price of bread. Again, instead of addressing the problem, Mugabe preferred to see it as an excuse to attack the MDC, which was particularly strong in that area. First, military helicopters bombed the crowds with canisters of tear gas, then trained soldiers of the Parachute Regiment, armed with clubs and whips, beat everyone they could lay their hands on. Their savagery did not spare the very young.

Now, led by Hunzvi, attacks began on Harare's white-owned businesses, including shops and hotels, even hospitals and aid organisations. However, the raiding of 18 South African companies was a step too far and Zimbabwe's High Commissioner in Pretoria was summoned for a severe reprimand. (On 4 June 2001, Hunzvi died in

Bulawayo of an AIDS-related condition and was promptly declared a 'national hero'.)

In January 2002, in the hope of driving the remaining whites out of the country, Mugabe abolished dual nationality. Forty thousand Zimbabweans of British origin opted to retain their British passports and only a few thousand, mainly from the younger generation, opted for a Zimbabwean passport. This meant that these 40,000 (of whom about 20,000 were pensioners) were technically no longer Zimbabwean citizens. However, although Mugabe was anxious to see them leave the country, the price of an air ticket to the UK because of the raging inflation had by then reached the staggering price of Z$1 million. This was beyond most people's means.

On 2 September 2002, Mugabe addressed the World Summit on Sustainable Development in Johannesburg. Economically, Zimbabwe, even 22 years after independence, was still an 'occupied country,' he maintained. Therefore, his government had decided to do 'the only right and just thing' by confiscating the land and 'giving it to its rightful, indigenous, black owners, who lost it in circumstances of colonial pillage'.

Zimbabwe was brought into the spotlight through sport when cricket's governing body the International Cricket Council (ICC), decreed that six matches of the Cricket World Cup (of which Zimbabwe, Kenya and South Africa were co-hosts) would be played in Harare and Bulawayo in February 2003; a decision considered by many to be one of appalling insensitivity. The greatest moment of the entire tournament was not Ricky Ponting's blistering 140 in the final but when Zimbabwean cricketers, (white) Andy Flower and (black) Henry Olonga, wore black armbands for their opening game, explaining they were 'mourning the death of democracy in our beloved Zimbabwe'. Both subsequently retired from Zimbabwean cricket and started playing and coaching overseas. A warrant was issued for Henry Olonga's arrest on charges of treason and he had to go into hiding for a while. The following year, Mugabe, a patron of the Zimbabwe Cricket Union, declared:

> Cricket civilises people and creates good gentlemen. I want everyone to learn cricket in Zimbabwe. I want ours to be a nation of gentlemen.

Here is part of the statement released by the two cricketers:

> We cannot in good conscience take to the field and ignore the fact that millions of our compatriots are starving, unemployed and oppressed. We are aware that hundreds of thousands of Zimbabweans may even die in

> the coming months through a combination of starvation, poverty and AIDS. We are aware that many people have been unjustly imprisoned and tortured simply for expressing their opinions about what is happening in the country. We have heard a torrent of racist hate speech directed at minority groups. We are aware that thousands of Zimbabweans are routinely denied their right to freedom of expression. We are aware that people have been murdered, raped, beaten and had their homes destroyed because of their beliefs and that many of those responsible have not been prosecuted ... It is impossible to ignore what is happening in Zimbabwe. Although we are just professional cricketers, we do have a conscience and feelings. We believe that if we remain silent that will be taken as a sign that either we do not care or we condone what is happening in Zimbabwe.

Thank you, gentlemen.

As mentioned briefly earlier, in May 2005, Mugabe's paramilitary police terrorised the inhabitants of the squatter camps around Bulawayo (most of whom had voted for the opposition MDC during the country's parliamentary elections held in March.) There followed 'Operation Murambatsvina' ('Operation Drive Out the Trash') in which Mugabe's henchmen forced the squatters to destroy their own dwellings, then looted everything of value and burnt what remained on a bonfire. His timing was intended to cause maximum hardship, for this was the middle of the Zimbabwean winter. A similar incident took place at Victoria Falls, where an estimated 30,000 people were evicted from their homes.[4] The United Nations declared that as many as 1.5 million people had been made homeless by this programme of Mugabe's, which he referred to as 'urban renewal'.

Mugabe continued his relentless persecution, his victims being predominantly the Ndebele people (together with the Kalanga, who are related to the Shona and inhabit the region to the south-west of Bulawayo) and those Shona who live in the poor suburbs of Harare. They had dared to oppose him (albeit democratically) by supporting Morgan Tsvangirai's opposition MDC. Every move they made (or make) to draw attention to their desperate plight was, and is, met with instant brutality. The violence of Mugabe's regime is not even commensurate with the perceived threat, it is always disproportionately extreme.

In June 2005, *Daily Mail* reporter Con Coughlin managed to gain access to the squatter communities on the outskirts of Bulawayo, even though Mugabe had banned western journalists from his country.

> The lucky ones live in mud huts that have been scraped together from the drought-afflicted dirt; the rest in haphazard constructions made out of detritus collected from the city's garbage dumps.
>
> Their pathetic possessions amount to a few ragged blankets; blackened pots and pans, and primitive, hand-made tools with which they attempt to cultivate a few subsistence crops from the barren soil.
>
> They live on one simple meal a day – a gruel-like substance made from boiled maize. With 80 per cent of Zimbabwe's population officially unemployed, their only source of income derives from selling their paltry goods on the city streets.

As Coughlin watched, the police looted what they could, before burning everything, including the bags of maize, upon which the destitute squatters and their families depended for their very existence. 'Great columns of black smoke stretched high into the vast expanse of the African sky.' He was witnessing at first hand 'Operation Murambatsvina'.

Similarly, in the capital Harare, about 200,000 people were driven from their homes at Hatcliffe Heights, Highfield and Kambuzuma. Three army battalions supported by helicopter gunships were used in this operation. Also, an estimated 30,000 people were evicted from their homes at Victoria Falls, the country's main tourist attraction. Mugabe's justification was that 'The current state of affairs in unregulated and crime-ridden areas could not have been tolerated for much longer … [This was] a vigorous clean-up campaign to restore sanity.' He explained:

> We removed them from slums and put them in new places. Obviously when you destroy slums, even as you prepare new places for them, there is dislocation, disorganisation of the family for that moment.[5]

This, of course, was an admission that no 'new places' had actually been prepared. The 'Trash' had been driven into the bush, there to scavenge like wild animals, to whom they themselves now became prey.

CLEAN UP

I can see clearly now
The shack is gone
I can see the stars
Quivering as if
Afraid of the dark.

I can see
The baleful moon
With clouds blowing
Across its distraught face,
Lonely as if
Bereaved.

I can smell the freshness
Of the garbage
The persistent breeze,
Like the tax man,
Insistent on its demands
On my body warmth.

Now I can see the dawn
Painting the sky
Blood red
The early warning
Of the visiting hunger.

I can feel the sun
Teasing me
With its morning warmth
That soon turns
To a scorching hate.

Now the compound
Is silent and mute,
I can hear distant calls
From lost children: a generation
With no past or future:
A mere memory lapse.

Chris Magadza, Harare, 2005

In an address to the United Nations in September 2005, Mugabe revealed that it was all a plot by the enemies of Zimbabwe:

> In the aftermath of our urban clean-up operation, popularly called 'Operation Murambatsvina', or 'Restore Order' – the familiar noises re-echoed from the same malicious prophets of doom, claiming that there

> was a humanitarian crisis in Zimbabwe. Those unfounded alarms are aimed at deliberately tarnishing the image of Zimbabwe and projecting it as a failed state.[6]

In November 2005, when international food agencies attempted to supply food to his starving population, Mugabe's response was, 'Why foist this food upon us? We do not want to be choked, we have enough.'[7]

A group who were particularly singled out by Mugabe for persecution were homosexuals, whom he described as, 'worse than dogs and pigs'; 'beasts' who were 'guilty of sub-human behaviour'.[8] (It is interesting to note that a study performed at the University of Cincinnati, USA in January 1994 indicates that a characteristic feature of homophobes is that they tend to have an intensely authoritarian view of life, and that they are also likely to be racists.)[9]

In January 2007, reporter RW Johnson described how, with normal growth, Zimbabwe's population would be calculated to stand at 18 million, if this were an average country in the developing world. As about four million had fled the country, this would, therefore, leave 14 million. However, social scientists estimated that the population of Zimbabwe was actually between eight and 11 million. In other words, between three and six million people were unaccounted for. If so, then this state of affairs would be entirely satisfying to Didymus Mutasa, Head of Zimbabwe's Secret Police, who had declared back in 2002: 'We would be better off with only six million people … We don't want all these extra people.'[10] A death rate of 10 per 1,000 in 1985 had leapt to a catastrophic 25 per 1,000 by 2002.

Mugabe once compared himself, unashamedly, to Hitler. Perhaps his own moustache is some kind of homage to one perceived as a kindred spirit:

> This Hitler has only one objective; justice for his people, sovereignty for his people, recognition of the independence of his people and their rights over their resources.[11]

If some of the missing millions in Mugabe's country have disappeared through genocide, the comparison is apt for very different reasons.

14

Mugabe's 'Jewel of Africa': Economic Meltdown and Social Disintegration

In order to understand fully the catastrophic effects of Mugabe's presidency, it is important to recall just what a strong and balanced economy he inherited when he first came to power.

In 1980, Zimbabwe was the world's largest exporter of white maize; its third largest exporter of tobacco, and the largest exporter of cotton and beef in Africa. Cotton, ground nuts, soya bean, sorghum, wheat, tea, coffee, sugar cane, fruit (including grapes) and vegetables were also important products. Livestock included some five million cattle, 400,000 sheep, 1.3 million goats, 150,000 pigs, together with poultry and bees. In 1981, 11,000 tons of fish were caught commercially from Lake Kariba.

In 1980, Zimbabwe was one of the world's largest producers of chrome, and the sixth largest producer of gold. Other important minerals which were mined included antimony, asbestos, barites, coal, copper, corundum, dolomite, emeralds, garnets, graphite, magnesite, nickel, phosphate, and steatite (soapstone).

Over 50 per cent of the country was under woodland or forest, the timber from which was in great demand – in particular, Rhodesian teak for parquet-flooring blocks, mukwa for plywood, and nchibi for furniture veneer. Other important industrial products included cement, fertiliser, steel, glass, paper, and rubber. In 1980, Zimbabwe had a surplus on its balance of trade of Z$100 million, excluding gold sales.

Tourists contributed substantially to the economy. They came for many reasons: to hunt, to play golf, to visit the game reserves, the Matopos, and the Inyanga National Parks; or the Vumba or Chimanimani Mountains.

Lake Kariba was created when a dam was built across the Kariba Gorge on the Zambesi river, 300 miles below the Victoria Falls. Since it

The fruits of the 'Jewel of Africa'; grain storage depot at Gwelo in the 1950s.

Empty supermarket shelves, Bulawayo, September 2007.

was opened in 1959, Kariba, as well as providing hydroelectric power, has become a Mecca for wildlife enthusiasts and fishermen, and also a playground for water sport enthusiasts.

Rhodesia's most famous and enigmatic monument, Great Zimbabwe, lies 70 miles to the south-east of Gwelo, near Fort Victoria. (Its name derives from the Shona 'dzimba dza mabwe', meaning 'houses of stone'.) When Great Zimbabwe was built, no one knows, nor who built it, for the original buildings pre-date the Bantu migration.

The Victoria Falls are surely the greatest riverine wonder of the world. On approach, the roar of the water – sounding like continuous thunder – can be heard from a distance of several miles. On closer approach, the

The mysterious
Zimbabwe ruins.

very earth beneath one's feet vibrates, as the rainbow, which shines overhead in the perpetual mist that the water throws up, comes into view. All of these riches — agriculture, industry, mining, forestry, tourist income — would be squandered and destroyed by Mugabe.

By 1990, by which time Mugabe had been in power for a decade, the economy of Zimbabwe was in sharp decline. He imposed artificial controls over prices, dividends and exchange rates, which caused foreign investment in the country virtually to cease. He chose to ignore a reform package put together by the International Monetary Fund (IMF), with the result that young people, having completed their studies, were released into a society where there were no jobs. By December 1999, with Zimbabwe having no remaining foreign exchange reserves, the IMF withdrew all support. As far as its international creditors were concerned, the country was now considered to be a bad risk, and no further loans were forthcoming.

Despite Mugabe's vitriolic rhetoric directed against Britain, America, and Europe, foreign aid continued to pour in. In 2002, the European Community (EC) allocated £83 million for food aid and another £5 million for 'ongoing development projects in direct support of the population in the social sectors', and in the fields of 'democratisation, respect for human rights and the rule of law'. The USA provided US$17.2 million for the treatment and prevention of disease caused by HIV, and for

Victoria Falls.

David Livingstone's statue, Victoria Falls.

micro-financial economic programmes.[1] Mugabe's response to this generosity was to declare haughtily, 'What do I need Europe for?' In the future, he would promote stronger ties with Asian states, such as Malaysia.

In May 2007, Mugabe announced plans to seize a majority stakeholding in all Zimbabwe's foreign-owned companies, the shares thus acquired by him to be given to 'indigenous' Zimbabweans, whom he defined as 'any person who was disadvantaged by unfair discrimination on the grounds of race before independence in 1980'.[2]

In June 2007, in a futile, almost childish effort to combat inflation, Mugabe imposed a total freeze on prices without reference to Parliament. This resulted in many shops and factories ceasing to operate, as they could not trade at a loss.[3] Even in the capital Harare, basic items such as meat, bread, cooking oil and soap now disappeared from the shelves. Mugabe's next move was to order Zimbabwe's businessmen to halve the price of their goods and services. He also warned them that, if they did not open for business as usual, their trading licences would be withdrawn and their businesses taken over. Of those who defied the order, sixteen – including supermarket and petrol station owners and a leading fashion retailer – were imprisoned. Another 2,000 were arrested and fined.[4] So much for Mugabe's economics degree.

With such economic meltdown came immense social distress. According to David Coltart of the MDC, an estimated 4,000 lives per week were being lost from starvation and from AIDS.[5] The fact that farms lay idle meant not only that no food was being produced, but also that an estimated 400,000 of their black Zimbabwean employees became unemployed. The United Nations Food Programme estimated that 4.1 million Zimbabweans would need food aid by the year 2008, otherwise they would face starvation.

Loveness Mangete, a teenager from Empandeni, west of Bulawayo, who was a Roman Catholic, made this pitiful statement:

> It is not just that we do not have any food in our homes or in our fields. But even if we have any money we cannot buy any food because the shops do not have anything, so what can we do? Perhaps the only thing is to pray.

Meanwhile, one of Zimbabwe's greatest tourist attractions, the game reserves, were in dire straits. Poaching was rife, which was not surprising in this land of starvation. In July 2007, the Zimbabwe Conservation Task Force (ZCTF) reported that, in sixty of the country's private game reserves, more than 90 per cent of the game had been lost to poachers – including endangered species such as the black rhinoceros and the wild dog.[6] Mugabe ordered 100 elephants to be slaughtered for a feast on Independence Day – 18 April 2007. The following month, the ZCTF estimated that 60 per cent of the country's wild animals had been killed since the launch of Mugabe's Land Reform Programme in 1992. Lauren St John, reporting for Britain's *Daily Mail*, stated that some rare species, including leopard, rhino, blue duiker (small antelope), cheetah, and African wild dog were being hunted to the brink of extinction.[7]

The tourist industry has been destroyed. Why would a person wish to visit Zimbabwe, which has become, in effect, not only a wasteland, but also a concentration camp, from which the majority of the inmates are desperate to escape, if they have not already done so?

In January 2007 it was reported that there were an estimated 1.3 million orphans in Zimbabwe; that 42,000 women had died in childbirth in the previous year (compared with fewer than 1,000 a decade before); that the mortality for the under-five age group was 132 per 1,000 (compared with 80 per 1,000 in 1990); that deaths from AIDS were running at 180,000 per annum (compared with 160,000 in 2001), and that the value of the Gross Domestic Product had fallen from US$7.4 billion in 2000, to US$3.4 billion in 2005. Only about 50 per cent of children of school age attend school (compared with 80 per cent in 1988.)[8] The former teacher turned tyrant is silent on the matter.

In August 2007, the World Health Organisation declared that the average life expectancy of a Zimbabwean woman was 34 years, and that of a man, 36 years (compared with 63 and 54 respectively a decade earlier).

Many Zimbabweans survive on money sent to them from friends and relatives living abroad. However, there is a price to pay, both for the donor and for the recipient. This is because, by Zimbabwean law, all foreign currency transactions are required to go through the Central Bank, which takes a substantial slice of such charitable donations.[9]

In 2007, Zimbabwe's inflation rate was the highest in the world at 7,600 per cent and its economy was shrinking faster than that of any other country. The balance of payments problem was critical, owing to a catastrophic decline in export earnings, and 80 per cent of the working population was unemployed. On 30 August, British Foreign Office minister Lord Maloch Brown announced that even China, who up until then had been a major supplier of military equipment to Zimbabwe, was now withdrawing all support, except for humanitarian aid.[10]

Contrast Mugabe's behaviour with that of his more enlightened neighbours: Malawi's Hastings Banda, Zambia's Kenneth Kaunda, and Mozambique's Samora Machel. All three leaders encouraged a good number of white civil servants and businessmen to remain at their posts in their newly independent countries, which would therefore benefit from their experience and expertise. Had Mugabe done the same, the catastrophe of Zimbabwe could surely have been avoided, for it was in everyone's interests, both black and white, that Zimbabwe should remain prosperous.

Was Mugabe's primary intention to ruin Zimbabwe? The answer, perhaps surprisingly in the light of what seems such wilful destruction, is no. His primary aim was to *punish those who opposed him*. Mugabe may be likened to an infant child who kicks his mother when he cannot get his own way. Is Mugabe capable of changing his ways? This question will be addressed shortly.

15

'Nhamodzenyika' – The Suffering Country

The name given by Mugabe to his only son, born in September 1963 to his first wife Sally, was 'Nhamodzenyika', which in Shona means 'the suffering country'. This was clearly a reference to Southern Rhodesia. But was the country suffering? The vast majority of whites – who had affluent or even luxurious lifestyles – definitely were not. However, it is often forgotten that there were also a significant number of so-called 'poor whites', those who were deficient in education and skills, who often found employment on the white farms as supervisors of black labour.

Those blacks who worked for government establishments, or for the larger businesses, received food, shelter, and clothing – though this fell far short of that enjoyed by whites. Elsewhere, however, it would be idle to pretend that a degree of exploitation and abuse did not take place of black by white. There were rumours that some employers, particularly in the rural areas, fed their black workers on little more than beans and mealie meal and that they made excessive demands for labour, even enforcing their will with the sjambock. It was not unusual to hear whites quoting from the Bible and interpreting such expressions as, 'Hewers of wood and drawers of water'[1] as relating specifically and solely to the blacks. This doctrine, of course, dovetailed conveniently with the doctrine of apartheid.

Although Guinea Fowl, a secondary school for whites near Gwelo (now Gweru) closed in 1978, it has a current website to which its former pupils contribute. To it, Simba Patrick Nyanhanga (who does not make it clear where he was educated) added the following, which indicates that his experience of white rule was deeply unpleasant, and that it left him feeling intensely outraged and bitter, quoted exactly:

> Rhodesian, it is very obvious you white colonial folkes do not and will never understand what Zimbabwe is. You may be a Boer, Dutch, Scot, Englishman, Canadian or any form of the descendants of the Great Trek folkes, you have had your days.
>
> All respects to your developments, but they werent ours. We are Zimbabwe, Blacks who accomodated you even when you robbed all we had, beat us up, abuse[d] us, made us slaves in our own land, yet you still remain to believe this can go to eternity.
>
> May your God help you, because you just got to our last straw of tolerence. Just open your eyes and revise what you had been doing to us all the previous years …
>
> Our spirit never dies, its simple, JOIN US AND RESPECT US OR JUST GET THE F … OUT OF OUR LAND. I believe in our Zimbabwe and in HOSTING you in a good manner as you appreciate and respect my hospitality. Always Black and Zimbabwean
>
> Simba Patrick Nyanhanga[2]

It was not only the blacks who saw the inherent injustices, which were present in Rhodesian society. Former white Rhodesian Michael Mellody of Gwelo, for example, stated that, in contrast with some other white ex-Rhodesians:

> I didn't think much of Rhodesia – probably because I was the only 'Rhodie' who didn't live in a fifty room house with two Olympic-sized swimming pools, five tennis courts, and twenty devoted servants. It was a strange, class-ridden, inbred, corrupt society which had all the bad traits of colonialism and few of the good.[3]

Although Southern Rhodesia's blacks were living as second-class citizens, nevertheless, the whites would argue, that they themselves were, in the main, well disposed towards them – in contrast with the situation in South Africa, where conditions for blacks were generally much harsher. In fact, visitors from South Africa often remarked on Southern Rhodesia's peaceful way of life, prosperity, and pleasant ambience. This was acknowledged by Mugabe himself, who on 3 March 1980, the month before independence, said to former Prime Minister Ian Smith, 'You have given me the jewel of Africa.'[4]

Any objective student of Zimbabwe today would have to agree that the situation now is infinitely worse for the vast majority of Zimbabwe's blacks (and of course for the whites too) than it was in postwar colonial times.

It is estimated that 3,500 people are dying each week from starvation, violence or disease.[5] The suffering is not all directly the result of Mugabe's brutality. It happens because the entire infrastructure of the country, so painstakingly built up over a century, has been allowed to crumble and decay.

In 2007, 300 children, all suffering from severe diarrhoea, were admitted to Harare's Central Hospital every week. This was the result of untreated sewage being diverted into Lake Chivero, the city's main water supply, Harare's sewage treatment plant having broken down. No drugs were available with which to treat these children, and their parents could only sit and watch as they died before their eyes.[6]

Many can only speak from beyond the grave, through the words of loving friends who have survived. One such person is 17-year-old Noel Sakala, who died from kidney failure in the state-run Mpilo Hospital in Bulawayo. He died because the kidney dialysis machine on which he was dependent had broken down and the hospital was unable to obtain the parts with which to repair it. Fifty-four more dialysis machines (all brand new and donated by the Government of Sweden in 2004) were never used because the expertise to maintain them, and the foreign currency required to purchase spare parts for them, does not exist.[7] Although it is a different African story from a different time, the words 'Cry, the Beloved Country' are evoked by such heartbreaking stories.

An unforgettable image of modern Zimbabwe is of people queuing for hours, sometimes days, to vote in elections which they are well aware will, in all probability, be rigged. Despite this, they show immense courage and vote for what they believe in, for what they know is right; even though, to vote for any party other than ZANU-PF means risking their lives and those of their families. Has any nation ever suffered more in the cause of democracy than Zimbabwe? Has any people appealed more to the outside world and been met with such indifference? One cannot help but reflect, bearing in mind what has gone on in the rest of the world, that had Zimbabwe been an oil-rich country, or one of strategic military importance, then Western governments would have taken steps to topple Mugabe long ago.

The world's press, despite Mugabe's attempts to deny it access to Zimbabwe, has shown many horrific images of its suffering people. One of the most poignant is that of its orphans: mournful, emaciated, huddled together on street corners, with only each other for company.

16

Self Aggrandisement: The Winner Takes All

In the mid-1980s, Mugabe, whose capacity for hypocrisy knew no bounds, declared:

> The people cannot be fooled for long into accepting ... those they judge to be self-aggrandising and seeking to enrich or benefit themselves at their expense.[1]

This expression of confidence in the democratic process was made whilst he and his ZANU-PF henchmen were grabbing everything they could lay their hands on. It was Mugabe's policy to distribute to his state officials, MPs, civil servants, police and military, the choicest of the farms which he had appropriated from their white owners. This meant that by 1990, eight per cent of commercial farmland was in the hands of his cronies. However, the new owners possessed neither the expertise, nor the motivation, to make the land productive. Farming in Central Africa is no easy matter, with hazards such as drought and voracious locusts to contend with.

In 1992, Mugabe's wife Sally died, and with the death of this humane and caring person, the final brake on his appalling behaviour was removed.

In April 1994, the month that the ANC won the South African elections and Nelson Mandela was elected President, the full extent of Zimbabwe's land appropriation scandal was exposed when an independent newspaper reported that a 3,000-acre farm had been purchased by the government, despite the white owner's objections, on the pretext that it was to be used for the resettlement of 33 homeless peasants. In fact, it was leased to Witness Mangwende, former Minister of Agriculture and then Minister of Education, as a reward for his having promoted the Land Acquisition Act. Further investigations revealed numerous other resettlement scandals in which the beneficiaries were invariably high-ranking officials loyal to Mugabe.

In December 1996, Brigadier Gibson Mashingaidze of ZANU-PF attended the funeral of impoverished war veteran Mukoma Musa, for whom he had paid Z$1,000 out of his own pocket in order to give Musa a decent burial. Even the brigadier was completely disillusioned:

> Some people now have ten farms to their names and luxury yachts, and have developed fat stomachs, when ex-combatants like Comrade Musa lived in abject poverty. Is this the ZANU-PF I trusted with my life?

In March 1997, the government was forced to suspend payments from the War Veterans' Compensation Fund, as the Z$450 million (equivalent to US$40 million) allocated for that year had been used up after only eight months. Pilfering by senior politicians and officials was suspected. When Margaret Dongo tabled a motion in Parliament, asking the Auditor-General to investigate the disappearance of the funds, more than 100 other MPs supported her, forcing Mugabe to appoint a commission of enquiry under High Court Judge Godfrey Chidyausiku to look into the matter. The judge confirmed that the system had, indeed, been grossly abused. A vivid example of such misappropriations was provided by Solomon Tawengwa, Executive Mayor of Harare, who was building himself a new mayoral mansion at a cost of Z$65 million, while the infrastructure of his city — its public health facilities, sanitation, hospitals and transport – was falling apart.

The assessor of claims made under the terms of the War Victims' Compensation Act, whereby former combatants were entitled to make claims for injuries sustained by them during the war for independence, was leader of the war veterans Chenjerai Hitler Hunzvi. Judge Chidyausiku discovered not only that the system was being grossly abused, but also that Hunzvi had awarded himself Z$517,536 for, 'impaired hearing' and, 'sciatic pains of the thigh'. Not to be outdone, the aptly named Reward Marufu, Mugabe's brother-in-law, was awarded Z$822,668 for, 'a scar on his left knee', and 'ulcers'! Numerous other high-ranking officials were paid similar amounts for conditions such as, 'skin allergy', 'polyarthritis', 'mental stress disorder', and so forth.[2] As Chakwana Mueri – 'Comrade Jesus' – was rewarded for his thuggish behaviour with a 1,000-acre tobacco farm, Mugabe declared an amnesty for all those who had committed political violence between January and July 2000.

On 18 March 2002, Terry Ford, a white farmer from Norton, 25 miles west of Harare, was attacked with axes by Mugabe's war veterans (many of whom were not war veterans at all) then run over and shot in the head. Pictures of his body covered in a blanket with his faithful dog sitting next to him were shown across the world. Ford's crime was to refuse to hand over his farm. He was the tenth white farmer to be murdered in the previous two years. Was it a coincidence that Mugabe's sister Sabina (MP for Zvimba, Mugabe's home district since 1985 and Finance Secretary for the ZANU-PF Women's League) had visited Ford 16 months earlier in her black Mercedes-Benz and informed him she required his farmstead for herself? Sabina's sons had their own rackets: the inappropriately named Innocent had been director of the government's repressive Central Intelligence Organisation (the Secret Police)[3] until his death in 2001, and Leo owned a consortium which obtained lucrative, no doubt inflated contracts for the construction of public buildings.[4]

The Times revealed that Mugabe had returned home from a lavish Christmas holiday in Thailand, Singapore and Malaysia. (Mugabe and his wife Grace had purchased a holiday home in Malaysia in 2005.) Incidentally, the state-owned airline Air Zimbabwe was £18 million in debt. On their return journey, ten seats of the aircraft were taken up by Mugabe's wife, children, and other 'camp followers', and no less than 15 trolleys, piled high with packages labelled 'State House, Harare' were loaded on board the aircraft, doubtless containing the fruits of a lavish spending spree.[5]

In late March 2007, Mugabe received the endorsement of ZANU-PF to stand for a further five-year term in the following year's elections.

Borrowdale Brooke suburb is the location of Mugabe's palatial hillside residence, built at an estimated cost of £8 million, complete with 25 bedrooms and extensive grounds containing two lakes. Its ceilings were designed by Arabic craftsmen, and its glazed, blue roofing-tiles were imported from China.[6] Mugabe also owns three farms: Highfield Estate in Norton, Ironmask Estate, and Foyle Farm in Mazoe (all of which were forcibly seized from their previous owners) together with a holiday home near Cape Town.

Also in Borrowdale are the mansions of Mugabe's highest ranking comrades from ZANU-PF and those of the country's most wealthy businessmen. Not surprisingly, in the local Spar supermarket, BBC correspondent John Berger discovered on a reconnaissance in 2006 that commodities were in plentiful supply: bread, sun-dried tomatoes, cigars and frozen foods including fish, shrimps and squid. He contrasted this with the TM Superstore at Chitungwiza on the other side of the city, where there was 'no bread, no fresh meat, no maize meal, but plentiful supplies of condiments, packet soups and lavatory paper'.

Grace Mugabe is known to have withdrawn the equivalent of more than £5 million from Zimbabwe's Central Bank over the past five years to finance her shopping jaunts.[7] How does Mugabe find the money to prop up himself and his regime? The answer is that the German company G&D (Giesecke & Devrient), which has printed the country's banknotes since the 1970s, simply prints it at the astonishing rate of Z$170 trillion a week!

> Some of this money was used to award huge pay rises to the army, in an apparent move to buy their loyalty ahead of the Presidential and Parliamentary Elections on March 29.[8]

A museum dedicated to the life and achievements of Mugabe is currently being built at a cost of £2 million in his home district of Zvimba. Exhibits will include letters he wrote during the period of his imprisonment, photographs dating from the time of the guerrilla war and copies of his speeches. There will also be a 16-foot-long stuffed Nile crocodile – a recent birthday present from his loyal ministers and officials.[9]

17
Lisbon: the Europe/Africa Summit

The Europe/Africa summit conference which began in the Portuguese capital of Lisbon on 8 December 2007 was the first for seven years, previous ones having been cancelled owing to a dispute over whether Mugabe, whom many African leaders regard as a hero, should be invited or not.

Under the terms of sanctions imposed on Zimbabwe in 2005, Mugabe was banned from travelling to all European countries. However, on this occasion, the European Union decided to invite him to the Lisbon Summit. The reaction by British Prime Minister Gordon Brown was immediate: neither he, nor any other senior British Government minister would attend the meeting in Portugal, although he would send Baroness Amos, former Leader of the House of Lords, to represent Britain.

A fortnight before the commencement of the summit, Mugabe's Press Secretary George Charamba declared that the British were 'contemplating the elimination of our political leadership through a number of assassinations' and that it was only Britain's fear of the firepower of Mugabe's forces that averted a British invasion.[1] On 21 November 2007, Ian Smith, Rhodesia's former Prime Minister, died at the age of 88.

At the summit, the subject of Zimbabwe did not appear on the agenda, presumably at the insistence of the other African leaders present. German Chancellor Angela Merkel, however, waded straight into the fray:

> The current state of Zimbabwe damages the image of the new Africa. Because this is so, we must take the chance here, in this framework, to put all our efforts together into strengthening democracy. We do not have the

> right to look away when human rights are trampled on. Intimidation of those with different opinions, and breaches of the independence of the Press, cannot be justified. We, the whole European Union, are united in our assessment … Zimbabwe's situation concerns us all, in Europe as well as in Africa.

Mugabe 'betrayed no emotion as Mrs Merkel spoke'.[2] Later, Mugabe enquired sarcastically 'Why is the Prime Minister of Great Britain not here?' before answering the question himself: 'Because he had his spokesman here from Germany.' Then, indulging in his old, familiar rhetoric, he described how Zimbabwe had endured a long struggle for democracy following almost a century of colonial oppression and declared that Europeans were convinced of their 'superiority over Africans'. As for accusations that his regime was guilty of abusing human rights, he described such charges as 'trumped up'.[3] The next speaker at the summit was President Thabo Mbeki of South Africa who scrupulously refrained from mentioning Zimbabwe.

At the conclusion of the Summit, Mugabe, along with other African leaders, signed the Lisbon Declaration, the stated objective of which was:

> To build a new strategic political partnership for the future, overcoming the traditional donor-recipient relationship, and building on common values and goals in our pursuit of peace and stability, democracy and the rule of law, progress and development.

If Angela Merkel believed for a moment that her attempts to shame Mugabe into changing his ways would have any effect, she was mistaken. If European and African delegates to the summit believed that Mugabe saw the Lisbon Declaration as having any kind of authority, they were equally wrong. Mugabe would now return home and continue, as he had always done, without changing his course one iota. In fact, he was *incapable of so doing*, for reasons which will be explained.

18

An Election is Called

In April 2007, colleagues from the Southern African Development Community (SADC), an organisation whose aims were to further socio-economic, political, and security cooperation between 15 Southern African countries (Zimbabwe included) handed the South African President Thabo Mbeki what reporter Aderogba Obisesan called a 'poisoned chalice'. Mbeki was given the task of mediating between Mugabe's ZANU-PF Party and the main opposition Movement for Democratic Change, with the object of establishing for Zimbabwe:

1. A framework for future presidential and parliamentary elections which were to be fairer and more open.
2. A new constitution for the country.
3. The repeal of its rigid and oppressive security laws.

In order to secure his position before any such changes could be put into effect, Mugabe announced on 2 February 2008 that there would be presidential, parliamentary, and local elections, commencing on 29 March.[1] It was a pre-emptive strike.

On 5 February 2008, 57-year-old Simbarashe (known as Simba) Herbert Stanley Makoni announced that he would challenge Mugabe for the presidency. Makoni was a seasoned politician. At Zimbabwe's independence in 1980 he had served Mugabe as Deputy Minister of Agriculture. He subsequently became Executive Director of the SADC. From 2000 to 2002, Makoni held the post of Minister of Finance and Economic Development in Mugabe's Cabinet. However, when he proposed that the Zimbabwean dollar be devalued, Mugabe disagreed and Makoni was dismissed from his post and replaced.

On 12 February 2008, Makoni was ejected from ZANU-PF. 'The rules are very clear,' said the Party's Secretary for Information and Publicity Nathan Shamuyarira, 'that anyone who tries to challenge an elected candidate of the Party stands expelled.'[2] Makoni would be obliged to run as an independent candidate. Launching his election manifesto, Makoni said:

> The Zimbabwe of today ... is a nation full of fear, a nation in deep distress, a tense and polarised nation, a nation also characterised by disease and extreme poverty.

He described the need for land reform as being more urgent than ever. Such reform would not be achieved by the seizure of land in an effort to redress the wrongs of the colonial era.[3] Makoni adopted a rising sun emblem for his campaign, declaring that it represented 'newness, light and hope for the regeneration and renewal of the Zimbabwean spirit'. He believed that Zimbabwe's problems were not intractable, and he promised to 'institute a future process of national healing and reconciliation'.[4]

> Let this not be a contest of fists, a contest of stones, knives and guns, but let it be a contest of ideas, a contest of vision and commitment to the people.[5]

Mugabe's reaction to Makoni's decision to challenge him was entirely predictable. He was incapable of responding to the challenge in a dignified and reasonable way, and as for producing a reasoned argument, Mugabe's cupboard was as bare as the shelves of the country's supermarkets. Speaking in a nationwide television broadcast on Thursday 21 February 2008, on his 84th birthday, Mugabe attacked with the only verbal weapon at his disposal – personal abuse:

> What has happened now is absolutely disgraceful. I didn't think that Makoni, after all the [his] experience, could behave like the way he did, and in a naïve way too. He does not have a party but he says that people should come to him. He is behaving like a magnet. Come to me and I am there to lead you. No! You go to the people and the people find you.
>
> So I have compared him to a prostitute. But you see a prostitute could have done better than Makoni because he has clients. A prostitute could have stood up also saying, 'I have boyfriends in the MDC, others are in

> ZANU-PF. There is no party without my boyfriends, so I am going to the nomination [court] as well.'

The homosexual smear was accompanied with a comparison of Makoni to his former Information Minister Jonathan Moyo, who had joined the Party and later deserted it. Such people, said Mugabe, using a favourite word of his, had become 'deviant'.[6]

Meanwhile, the leaders of the larger factions of the MDC, Morgan Tsvangerai, and of its smaller faction, Arthur Guseni Oliver Mutambara, declared that they would run separately in both the presidential and parliamentary polls.

On Saturday 23 February 2008, Mugabe threw a party at the border town of Beitbridge to mark his 84th birthday. Those invited included members of his ruling ZANU-PF party, chiefs, diplomats, government ministers, and his wife Grace and their children.

To swell the numbers, local villagers were forced onto buses and driven to Beitbridge, and beaten if they refused to cooperate. Doubtless, when they arrived, they were grateful for the free food which was on offer.

A laughing Mugabe, wearing a garland of flowers and surrounded by supporters, was seen characteristically punching the air with his fists, and skipping gleefully along to the sound of piped music.

Mugabe used the occasion to launch his campaign for a sixth term in office. He attacked his country's 'enemies', including the USA and Britain, who had criticised his presidency. 'There will never be regime change here, never,' he declared, a clear indication that if the forthcoming elections went against him, he would ignore the results. To members of his ruling party, he said:

> Let's tell people the truth about the economic hardships they are facing; the truth about what government is able to do and what it is not able to – as if they did not know already! We are going to work hard to address the problem.[7]

By then, inflation exceeded 100,000 per cent and a loaf of bread cost 1 million Zimbabwean dollars, or one third of the average daily wage.

Mugabe predicted that ZANU-PF would win the forthcoming election 'resoundingly', and insisted that he was not responsible for Zimbabwe's woes.[8] The state radio engaged in an unusual propaganda blitz, praising Mugabe as the nation's founding father. Not to be outdone, the state Press described Mugabe as 'a visionary and an exemplary statesman'.[9] However, on the other side of the Limpopo river in the Republic of South Africa, anti-Mugabe demonstrators were making their presence felt. The message to him, inscribed on a large helium balloon which they launched into the sky, was:

> Bob, you've had your cake. Now beat it!

Two days later, on 25 February 2008, Mugabe hurled more personal insults at Makoni: 'He is like a frog trying to inflate itself up to the size of an ox. It will burst.'[10] He predicted a landslide victory, one which would be a severe blow to British Prime Minister Gordon Brown, who advocated regime change in Zimbabwe:

> I do hope that the humble pies – and they will be big ones – that we will deliver for the edification of the opposition, will be eaten and eaten satisfactorily.[11]

On 25 February 2008, the Global Zimbabwe Forum (which is concerned with social, economic, and political issues) issued an appeal:

> We ... call upon SADC and Africa in general to ensure that the elections [in Zimbabwe] are held in accordance with the expectations of the SADC protocol on elections, that was adopted in Mauritius in August 2004.

This was a reference to a summit conference. What were the chances? None, because torture and intimidation of the electorate was not something which occurred solely at election times, as Tendai Chabvuta, Head of the Research Department of Zimbabwe's Human Rights NGO Forum pointed out:

> It is quite clear that 2007 is the worst year for human rights, in terms of politically motivated violence against opposition forces and human rights activists.[12]

The Forum reported in excess of 6,000 instances of human rights abuses in the country in the year 2007. In addition, reporter Stephen Bevan described how an investigation by The *Sunday Telegraph* had revealed that torture was no longer the sole preserve of the feared Central Intelligence Organisation (Zimbabwe's internal security agency). Now, such methods were 'routinely employed by uniformed police officers'.

Bevan reported that Fairbridge Camp, for example, situated 15 miles from the city of Bulawayo, acted as:

> … a regional interrogation centre for students and protest leaders arrested in Southern Zimbabwe – where support for the MDC is strongest. Its bloodstained cells had been full in recent months.

19

Intimidation, Dirty Tricks, Propaganda

Mugabe had largely outmanoeuvred his political opponents well before the elections were held, simply by driving the bulk of the electorate who would have voted against him out of the country. This fact was pointed out by Britain's Minister of State at the Foreign and Commonwealth Office with responsibility for Africa, Lord Malloch-Brown, who stated that these 4 million Zimbabweans were 'essentially disenfranchised'.[1]

As far as the composition of the Zimbabwe Electoral Commission (ZEC) which would monitor the forthcoming elections was concerned, again, Mugabe was in the driving seat; for his spokesman George Charamba declared that only observers from countries or organisations that had *not criticised* Zimbabwe's past elections would be invited to be monitors. Among those countries, 47 in all, which were considered likely to be sympathetic to Mugabe's cause, were the members of the SADC (including South Africa), Ethiopia, Nigeria, China, Iran, Venezuela, Kenya, Sudan and Libya, many of them having appalling human rights records themselves, and the Kenyan Government having been accused of massive vote rigging in its own election of December 2007. The European Union, said Charamba, would definitely not be invited to send observers to the forthcoming election. Though there would be, in addition, internal observers, from NGOs such as 'Zimbabwe Democracy Now'.

About 300,000 tonnes of maize, supplied to Zimbabwe by Malawi's President Bingu wa Mutharika, was hoarded by ZANU-PF at Grain Marketing Board depots around the country. This would be distributed to those of the electorate who undertook to vote for Mugabe and his Party.[2]

One plank of Mugabe's 'campaign' was to blame shopkeepers for raising prices in order to turn voters against him. 'Some [shopkeepers] are saying, "Let's make life hard for the people so that they cry and blame it on Mugabe's government".'[3] In an open piece of bribery, Mugabe offered regional farming districts 500 tractors, 20 combine harvesters, 50,000 ox-drawn ploughs, 60,000 oxcarts, together with cattle, generators and diesel fuel – all paid for, allegedly, with money seized from private companies and aid agencies.[4]

A Mugabe election poster, in which he was depicted in an aggressive and menacing pose with fist raised in a ZANU-PF salute, reflected what was in store for those who opposed him. Its slogan was 'Get Behind the Fist'. Another bore the mystifying message 'Our Words, Our Sovereignty' and was signed 'Comrade RG Mugabe'.

Opposition posters were not tolerated. Amnesty International, for example, amongst the many cases of intimidation which it has cited, recorded an incident in which three MDC activists were forced not only to tear down their posters, but to eat them.

The disingenuous Mugabe preferred to fight the election not on issues which concerned the electorate, such as 'Where is my next meal to come from?' or 'Will I manage to get through another day without being beaten up by Mugabe's thugs?' but on those of his own choosing. And the issues that he chose had absolutely no relevance to the Zimbabwe of today. He preferred, for example, to portray the election as a fight against Britain. This explains why his election posters carried the slogans 'Revolution, yesterday, today, tomorrow'[5] suggesting that Zimbabweans should rise up and throw off the non-existent colonial yoke. 'Hey, hey, we are ready for a fight, a fight against the British. We will deal them a final blow,' he trumpeted. 'Our national sovereignty is not negotiable ... Zimbabwe will never be a colony again.'

The opposition posters were far more to the point. On one of them, worthless Zimbabwean bank notes had been stuck, with the tag line 'Starving Billionaire'.

In what was another distraction from the main business of the day, Mugabe chose to re-ignite the hoary old controversy of the white-owned farms, of which only about 200 remained. (These farms were, in size, only a fraction of what they had once been: portions of their land having been sliced off and reallocated to Mugabe's henchmen.) 'The land is ours, it must not be allowed to slip back into the hands of whites,' said Mugabe, as if this was in any way possible On Saturday, 5 April 2008, gangs of war veterans were therefore deployed once again against the white farms – the real aim of the exercise being, apart from its propaganda value, to offer this land in exchange for votes. Two black farmers were also among those whose farms were invaded because they had failed to support the ruling party.

Deon Theron, Vice-President of the Commercial Farmers' Union, refused to cooperate and was put on trial at Harare's Magistrates Court on a charge of trespassing on a farm which he bought 24 years ago, for which he faced a two-year prison sentence!

Mugabe announced that he intended to take control of one of the very last remaining sources of wealth – the country's foreign companies (70 of which were British owned) which included mines and banks. He intended to call a meeting with the leaders of these industries, and if they failed to reduce prices as he desired, then they would be nationalised:

> We are going to read the riot act to them. If they refuse, we will also not cooperate. We are going to use the Indigenisation and Empowerment Act which stipulates that all companies, be they mines or manufacturing companies, with foreign ownership, without black shareholders or with black shareholders without a majority, should have at least 51 per cent shares reserved for indigenous people.[6]

Mugabe signed the Act – which also conferred the ownership of tractors, generators, fuel and livestock seized from white farms on new black owners on the weekend of 8/9 March 2008.[7]

These distractions all provided Mugabe with an excuse to avoid discussions about why his leadership had been so disastrous; why the national debt had risen to 4.4 billion US dollars, and why 80 per cent of his people were living below the poverty line and were in despair.

20

The March 2008 Election: Further Skullduggery

Mugabe conducted his election campaign, attired as was his custom in a brightly coloured shirt with scarf in the colours of the Zimbabwean national flag and baseball hat of green, pink, and black. He was now showing his age. His speech was slow and slightly slurred, his eyelids drooped, and his eyes – expressionless and cold as ever – exhibited signs of 'arcus senilis' – discoloration of the periphery of the cornea.

As if to emphasise that he had taken no notice of German Chancellor Angela Merkel's criticism of him at the Lisbon Summit, Mugabe opened his 2008 election campaign by ridiculing the idea, when it was put to him, that he had rigged elections. 'They want to tell lies, lies.'[1] When he had cast his vote in his Harare constituency, the lies were flowing: 'We don't rig elections. We have that sense of honesty. I cannot sleep with my conscience if I have cheated in elections.'[2]

On 25 February 2008, *The Zimbabwean* newspaper carried details of a report from the Zimbabwean Human Rights Association to the effect that Chitungwiza – a dormitory town 20 miles from Harare – the suburbs of Manyame Park, Zengezh, and St Mary's, were all under an unofficial curfew, with police banning night-time meetings:

> Scores of opposition supporters in the rural areas are being forced to renounce their allegiance to the opposition MDC, or to the new presidential aspirant Makoni. They are being told that the MDC was a party for whites, backed by the British, and they have to be paraded at ruling party rallies, announcing that they are rejoining ZANU-PF.

Those who failed to do so were beaten with canes and knobkerries.[3] On Friday, 28 March 2008, the eve of the election, the streets of Harare were crammed with forty or so armoured vehicles and six Armoured Personnel Carriers. Mugabe had previously warned the opposition:

> If they make a disturbance, like in Kenya, you will see. We are not joking. We warn the MDC, if they want to put a rope around their necks that is OK.

For his election campaign, Mugabe had the benefit of two helicopters. Not so the opposition. On 25 March 2008, Brent Smyth, pilot of the helicopter which was due to take Tsvangari on a series of election rallies, was arrested in Harare and his helicopter impounded.

Theresa Makoni, the MDC candidate for Harare North, discovered that a large tent, purporting to be a polling booth, had been erected in an empty field: 8,450 people were registered to vote there, 'Where are the voters?' she enquired, for there was no one living in that vicinity. Makoni also discovered that over 8,000 people were registered to vote at the Glen Hat Housing Cooperative – an area of bushland where no one actually lived.

Zimbabwe's voters' roll contained the names of people long since dead, including Desmond Lardner-Burke, Minister for Law and Order prior to Independence, who died almost 30 years before. His name appeared for the Mount Pleasant Ward. Other people long gone appeared on Harare's Electoral Roll, including Fodias Kunyepa, born in 1901 and Rebecca Armstrong, born in 1900. The most notable name on the roll, was that of former Premier Ian Douglas Smith, who died in November 2007.

Mugabe declared that, even if the opposition won the election, he would never allow it to take power. In his own words, printed by the The *Herald* newspaper:

> You vote for them [MDC], but that will be a wasted vote. You will be cheating yourself as there is no way we can allow them to rule this country.

And as to Morgan Tsvangarai himself:

> Those who want to vote for him can do so, but those votes will be wasted votes. It will never happen as long as we are alive.[4]

At a rally in Harare, he reiterated to the crowd that Tsvangarai would 'never, never rule this country.'

On the morning of 29 March 2008, in the village of Concession, Ibbo Mandaza, Simba Makoni's Chief Strategist, discovered a government lorry loaded with postal votes. According to the MDC, 60,000 ballot papers for postal votes had been printed, when only about 20,000 voters were eligible for such votes.[5]

The opposition accused Mugabe of cramming the voters' roll with the names of people who did not exist. It also accused him of printing nine million ballot papers for an electorate which numbered only 5.9 million. Often, on a voters' roll, the same name was repeated on several occasions, or a voter's name would appear in different rolls.[6]

On the day of the elections, Saturday 29 March, about 11,000 polling stations were due to open at 7 a.m. As they did so, Air Force jets circled menacingly, in the sky. When voting commenced, large numbers of people were refused entry to the polling booths – on the grounds that either their names were not on the voters' roll, or that they did not possess the correct identification. Furthermore, they discovered the police had been given new powers (under the pretext of assisting the elderly and infirm) to venture right inside the polling booths.

The following day the polling stations began to post the results for the number of votes cast in the elections on their walls. For Mugabe and ZANU-PF, to allow this degree of transparency was a huge risk to take and it is highly unlikely that they would have done it voluntarily. It was probably a condition imposed upon them as a result of the previous SADC meeting in Mauritius.

MDC observers throughout the country collected the results as they appeared – which in the age of the mobile telephone, the digital camera and the computer was not difficult to do. The MDC began announcing results. To their great delight, they indicated that the MDC was in the lead. From that time on, the ZEC, presumably under pressure from Mugabe, deliberately reduced the publication of the results from its 'National Command Centre' in Harare to a trickle.[7]

Wednesday, 2 April brought more bad news for Mugabe, who had not been seen in public since the previous week-end, when his ZANU-PF Party announced the unthinkable: that it had lost control of the Lower House of Parliament, the opposition having gained 105 seats, ZANU-PF 93, with only twelve seats left to be counted. (The final, official tally was MDC 99 seats, ZANU-PF 97, the minority MDC faction 10, and independents one.) In addition, the MDC's observers discovered that Mugabe's Vice-President Joyce Majuru and his Ministers for Defence, Public Affairs, Justice, and Information had all lost their seats! The ZEC was quick to refute the MDC's news about Majuru, however, and declared that she had in fact won her seat after all.

But what about the vitally important Presidential Election poll? Once again, the MDC was first to declare the result. Tsvangarai had won 50.3 per cent of the vote and Mugabe 43.8 per cent, the remaining 5.9 per cent going to Makoni. As the threshold for a first-round win was 50 per cent of the vote, Tsvangarai had won! Several days later, however, the ZED had still not released the results of the Presidential Election officially – in 2005, the results were announced within 24 hours of the end of polling. As for the results of the Senate (Upper House) election, the ZEC decided to postpone publication for 'logistical' reasons.

Who could Mugabe blame for this humiliation? He had driven an estimated 4 million would-be voters out of the country, all of whom would, given the chance, have voted for the opposition. He had also used every underhand trick in the book to prevent others from expressing their democratic rights; despite this, he had lost.

Mugabe was hard-wired to lash out, find someone to blame. He could hardly arrest those members of the ZEC who were foreign nationals. What he could do, however, was to arrest those of its members who were Zimbabwean citizens, which he did, on 7 April 2008, when seven officials of the ZEC were arrested. At the same time, ZANU-PF claimed that the vote had been rigged.[8]

On 14 March 2008, Mr Justice Tendai Uchena, doubtless 'leaned on' by Mugabe, rejected the MDC's demand for the immediate publication of the election results. Now, even before the official results of the Presidential Elections had been announced, Mugabe and his Politburo demanded the election be re-run.

David Blair, reporting for *The Daily Telegraph*, pointed out under a Presidential Powers Act, passed as a 'temporary measure' in 1986, Mugabe had given himself powers to amend any law at will. He might, therefore, 'employ this device to delay a second round for weeks or months.'[9]

21

Zimbabwe in the World Spotlight

Zimbabwe was now in the world spotlight as never before, largely because so many countries were playing a part in events there, members of SADC in particular. The United Nations was also involved. Mugabe had accused Joshua Nkomo of being a snake: now, he himself was in the proverbial cleft stick – used in Africa to catch snakes. If he published the results of the Presidential Election without tampering with them, they would undoubtedly show he had lost, otherwise he would have done it already. If he continued to fail to publish them, then people would assume that he had something to hide. If he deliberately falsified the results – which it had undoubtedly crossed his mind to do – then he would be confronted with photographic evidence of results posted at each and every polling station, samples of which had already appeared in newspapers and on television screens throughout the world. Such evidence, of course, could also be supplied by the MDC, and by others – possibly even members of SADC themselves – those that had a conscience, that is.

On 12 April 2008, a summit conference of the SADC was held in Zambia. Within the ranks of the SADC, Zambia, Malawi, and Botswana appeared anxious for Mugabe to step down. Not so Thabo Mbeki of South Africa:

> If nobody wins a clear majority, the law provides for a second run. If that happens, I wouldn't describe it as a crisis.

If the original 29 March ballot had been free and fair, and the results published, this would have been true. This, however, was Zimbabwe under Mugabe, and the barriers to democracy were manifold:

1. The unfairly conducted elections of 29 March 2008.
2. The failure of the ZEC to publish the results of these elections.
3. The sickening violence which ZANU-PF continued to perpetrate against the MDC, even after the elections have taken place, in an exercise called 'Operation Where Did You Put Your Cross.'
4. The inevitability of Mugabe unleashing yet another wave of violence and terror on the MDC, in the event of another ballot being held.

Thabo Mbeki was well aware of this. Why, therefore, did he not convert his self-professed 'quiet diplomacy' to a more vigorous intervention, when a word from him would bring Mugabe at once to heel? Could it be that, given the powerfulness of his position, Mbeki was not only prepared to tolerate the violence in Zimbabwe, but tacitly to condone it?

Like Mugabe, ZANU-PF has a great deal to answer for. And how could any party, knowing that their leader had blood on his hands, put him forward for the presidency of Zimbabwe? The answer is obvious. ZANU-PF, as the instrument of Mugabe's will, was also steeped in blood. If Mugabe was no longer leader, who would protect them from possible subsequent charges of crimes against humanity?

On the same day, 12 April 2008, 54-year-old Tapiwa Mubwanda, a district chairman from Hurungwe West, Mashonaland, became the first MDC party official to be killed. He was beaten to death at his home. His wife and brother were also beaten and left in a serious condition.[1]

What would the late President Samora Machel of Mozambique have made of the present situation? Surely he would have found it ironic that his country (along with Zambia and Nigeria) is now benefiting from the expertise of many of Zimbabwe's former white farmers, which it had welcomed with open arms. Machel had advised Mugabe to work with the whites, and especially with the white farmers. One country's loss is another's gain.

On 16 April 2008, the Associated Press issued the following report from Harare: 'Zimbabwe Doctors for Human Rights said it had treated 174 cases of injuries consistent with assault and torture since the vote, including 17 on Wednesday. Most victims this week suffered multiple fractures.' The 'Wednesday' was 16 April, the day after the MDC, demanding the results of the Presidential Elections, had organised a nationwide strike. The Zimbabwe Lawyers for Human Rights painted a similar picture, reporting that two people had been killed and 29 hospitalised with serious injuries in dozens of attacks.

On the same day, SW Radio Africa (London) carried a report by Tichaona Sibanda, which called into question South African President

Thabo Mbeki's 'quiet diplomacy', and also his personal integrity. China, said Sibanda, had secretly shipped tens of thousands of small arms to the Zimbabwe Defence Forces in a Chinese-registered vessel the *An Yue Jiang*, via the South African port of Durban. Sibanda's report was based on information supplied that day by Martin Welz, editor of *Noseweek* – a Durban-based investigative magazine – to SW Radio Africa's 'Newsreel' programme. The shipping documents in question were in his possession and they showed that the arms had been purchased from a Chinese arms company called Poly Technologies, based in Beijing, and that they were destined for the Ministry of Defence, Causeway, Harare.

How does Zimbabwe pay China for its armaments? Not with Zimbabwean dollars, for these are virtually worthless. The only commodities which China could possibly want from Zimbabwe are raw materials such as minerals, which are undoubtedly, shipped to that country via South Africa.

The *An Yue Jiang* was in dock in Durban between 10th and 13th April. Her cargo included three million rounds of ammunition for Chinese-made AK47 assault rifles, 1,500 rocket-propelled grenades and 3,500 mortar bombs.

On 17 April, an article by David Christianson for *Business Day* (Johannesburg) stated that the *An Yue Jiang* was owned by the Chinese Ocean Shipping Company. The article described how the legality of the shipment had been called into question by South Africa's Democratic Alliance Party's spokesperson on defence, Rafeek Shah. Shah had pointed out that South Africa's National Conventional Arms Control Act prohibits exporting arms to conflict zones. Did that act not also prohibit the trans-shipments of arms to conflict zones?

Had these shipments of arms by China (which, it was thought, had withdrawn its support for Mugabe and his regime) and their transportation across South Africa to their Harare destination been going on for some time? If so, then Mbeki, whilst allegedly pursuing his policy of achieving peace and a fairer society in Zimbabwe, had in fact been facilitating Mugabe's repression of his people by force of arms.

Did not Mbeki see how his and his country's status on the world stage would be considerably enhanced were he to show real leadership in this crisis, by recognising that Mugabe's activities must be urgently curtailed?

Why did the USA and the West not put more pressure on Mbeki to face up to his regional responsibilities? There appear to be three principal reasons. Firstly, South Africa is of strategic and military importance to them. Secondly, South Africa is an arena of competition for influence between the USA and the West on the one hand, and such countries as

China, Malaysia, South Korea, and Brazil on the other. Thirdly, the USA and the West were the major investors in South Africa. In 2004, foreign investment in South Africa was as follows:

United Kingdom	42.8 per cent
USA	22.1 per cent
European Union	23.0 per cent

There were risks involved in upsetting Mbeki.

On 17 April 2008, on the BBC's Six O'Clock News programme, a Zimbabwean human rights expert referred to simply as 'Charles' (for obvious reasons) gave an eye-witness account of Mugabe's continued persecution of his people, even after the election. Charles had accompanied a friend to hospital in Harare, where people had journeyed from as far away as 200 km, in order to receive treatment.

> They had been beaten up, burned; some had ribs broken. Some of them had big wounds, like they had been exposed to physical torture or been exposed to heat of some kind.

Later that day, Tsvangirai, speaking on BBC Radio's 'World Tonight' programme from neighbouring Botswana – where he had taken refuge for his own safety – revealed that the day after the election, he was approached by ZANU-PF representatives. In return for the party persuading Mugabe to step down, they suggested the MDC join with them in a government of national unity. Tsvangirai would be permitted to choose from a panel of candidates for the new government, in which members of ZANU-PF were to be included. Five days later, ZANU-PF had a change of heart.

Tsvangirai also revealed that he had told the SADC at their meeting in Zambia on 12 April 2008 that the MDC had won the election, and therefore he could not entertain his participation in a 'run off' against Mugabe. Tsvangirai was also critical of Zimbabwe's southern neighbour: 'Should South Africa have taken a definitive position, we would have solved the problem of Zimbabwe.' Tsvangirai now felt, quite understandably, that Mbeki had no further useful part to play and that the time had come for his role as mediator in the Zimbabwean crisis to be terminated and that he should be replaced by the SADC's chairperson, Zambia's President Levi Mwanawasa. Said Tsvangirai, politely but firmly: 'We want to thank President Mbeki for all of his efforts, but [he] needs to be relieved of his duties.'

Apart from enabling him to cling on to power, there was another advantage for Mugabe in procrastinating over the election results. The delay gave him an ideal opportunity to continue with the persecution of his people. In the vain hope that his evil deeds would go unnoticed, he arranged for this torture to be performed mainly at night in the rural areas (as he had done in previous elections.)

QUIET DIPLOMACY

Of oil wells nor nuclear programmes,
Fundamentalists
Nor drug barons
We boast not.

Our terrorism is
Homegrown
For domestic
Consumption
With no export value.

Torture and mutilations
We cover with
State media,
Lest we be confused
For Sierra Leone,
Or Rwanda or Dafur.

Massacres and geonocide
We package
With blue ribbons
As souvenirs
For Africa summits:
No United Nations
Tribunals here.

No genital mutilation
Nor Sharia stonings
But AIDS-propagating rape
Is the daily ritual
Of our girls … and

Their mothers
To the obligate attendance
Of their sons
And husbands.

Blow upon blow,
To the deafening applause
Of the African Union,
We silently bare the pain
In the amphitheatre
Of quiet diplomacy.

God bless Africa.
God bless Zimbabwe.

Chris Magadza, Harare, 2004

On 18 April 2008, at celebrations marking 28 years of independence, Mugabe made his first speech since the election. He had nothing new to say:

> Do you want the British to come back? Do you want to be ruled by the British? You saw what happened when they heard the MDC had won. They all came from Canada and Australia and are waiting in our hotels. I want to warn you. It will never happen in this country.

What relevance these two countries had to the present situation is not clear. Britain's last vestige of legal control over Canada had ended in 1982, and her last vestige of authority over Australia had ended with the Australia Act of 1986. Nonetheless, it was 'Down with the British. Down with thieves who want to steal our country.'

Tsvangirai described 18 April 2008 as 'the saddest Independence Day'. However, on that day, a tiny, but bright chink of light appeared on the horizon, when dockers at the port of Durban openly defied the South African Government's position concerning the Chinese-registered vessel *An Yue Jiang*. Said Randall Howard, General Secretary of the South African Transport and Allied Workers Union (SATAWU):

> SATAWU does not agree with the position of the South African Government not to intervene with this shipment of weapons. Our members employed at Durban Container Terminal will not unload this

> cargo; neither will any of our members in the truck-driving sector move this cargo by road.[2]

This must have gladdened the heart of Tsvangirai, himself a former trade union leader, who would have been all the more gratified to know that on 20 April the *An Yue Jiang* was said to have left South African territorial waters, her cargo still on board.

On that day, MDC Secretary-General Tendai Laxton Biti declared that following the March elections, Zimbabwe was 'in a war situation'. Ten people had been killed, hundreds injured, and thousands displaced, driven from their homes.

(Later Tendai Biti would be arrested, and Zimbabwe's High Court would dismiss an application by the opposition for his release from detention. In addition to being charged with treason, the police would also charge him with 'causing dissatisfaction to the security forces', and with stating that 'Mugabe is an evil man who should be arrested and handed over to the Hague'.)

Carolyn Norris of Human Rights Watch said:

> What we have been identifying are camps, set up by ZANU-PF militia and others very close to the ruling party, to punish people for having voted for the opposition party. People are taken there at night, held for several hours, beaten with wooden planks or other wooden batons, and left by the side of the road.[3]

Although the results of the parliamentary elections had been officially declared, they clearly did not suit ZANU-PF. The party said that it was not happy with the tallying process and it demanded a recount in 23 constituencies. Whereupon, the ZEC's Chairman Justice George Chiweshe announced that the votes cast in the Presidential and Local Council Elections would *also* be recounted.

Had the results of the Presidential Poll been officially announced by the ZEC prior to ZANU-PF's request for a recount, then the ZEC's action might have been construed as reasonable. However, in affirming that the Presidential votes were to be recounted, *even though they had not yet been officially declared*, the outside world can only suspect that there has been collusion between ZEC and ZANU-PF. The MDC was adamant. It regarded this proposed recount of votes by the ZEC as illegal.

In August, China is to host the 2008 Olympic Games. According to the Olympic Charter, one of the 'Fundamental Principles of Olympism' is:

> ...to create a way of life based on the joy of effort, the educational value of good example, and respect for universal fundamental ethical principles.

The Charter states that the goal of Olympism is to promote 'a peaceful society concerned with the preservaton of human dignity'. Are sport and politics two entirely separate entities which may be conveniently compartmentalised, according to the prevailing circumstances? The Olympic Charter indicates that they are not.

Are the Chinese ignorant of what is going on in Zimbabwe? In the main, yes, because China is not a free country. However, the Chinese leadership is undoubtedly aware of *exactly what is* going on in that beleaguered country. It is incumbent upon China, this great and emerging world power, to set an example by putting its house in order. Desirable as the concept of economic growth may be, this should not be at the cost of unimaginable human suffering.

Meanwhile, Zambia's President Mwanawasa, showing a degree of leadership and independent thinking which had, hitherto, been sadly lacking in the members of the SADC, urged African countries not to allow the *An Yue Jiang* to dock in their ports.

22

Zimbabwe's Agony Continues

On 22 April 2008, Jacob Zuma, Deputy President of South Africa's ANC, met British Prime Minister Gordon Brown, after which the two men issued a joint statement:

> We resolved on the crisis in Zimbabwe to redouble our efforts to secure early publication of the election results. We call for an end to any violence or intimidation and stressed the importance of respect for the sovereign people of Zimbabwe and the choice they have made at the ballot box.

More words that Mugabe was to ignore, as he ignored the international protests of 2000, 2002, and 2005, when he engaged in similar violence to dissuade his people from voting the wrong way. In fact, having got away with it so often on previous occasions, his campaign of violence would now assume even more terrifying proportions.

On 23 April, it was the turn of the Evangelical Fellowship of Zimbabwe, the Catholic Bishops' Conference, and the Zimbabwe Council of Churches to issue a joint statement:

> Organised violence, perpetrated against individuals, families, and communities who are accused of campaigning or voting for the 'wrong' political party … has been unleashed throughout the country. We warn the world that if nothing is done to help the people of Zimbabwe from their predicament, we shall soon be witnessing genocide similar to that experienced in Kenya, Rwanda, Burundi, and other hot spots in Africa and elsewhere.

There are those who would argue that genocide – defined as the mass extermination of a particular group of human beings – had already begun.

Many of the older generation of Zimbabweans – Mugabe included – were brought up and educated in mission schools, and many of today's Zimbabweans continue to embrace the Christian faith and to attend church. How many times, in their terrible and protracted suffering, must they have been reminded of the words of Psalm 121:

> I will lift up mine eyes unto the hills, from whence cometh my help.

Once, Mugabe himself came over the hills, when he returned to his home country from Mozambique following the guerilla war. However, he did not bring help. Instead, he brought fire and the sword.

'Suffer little children to come unto me, and forbid them not: for of such is the kingdom of God,' said Jesus, according to the Gospel of St Luke.[1] 21-month-old Jessy Sazukwa, who on 24 April 2008 was lying asleep in a Zimbabwe hospital, was far from the kingdom of God; her home on a farm formerly owned by whites having been burned down by ZANU-PF youths.[2]

'Honour thy father and thy mother: that thy days may be long upon the land which the Lord thy God giveth thee.' Mugabe, no doubt, was taught this as a child.[3] On 23 April, the BBC news showed an 84-year-old female MDC supporter with a head wound above her right eye. She was staggering, but being helped along by two friends. She had been struck on the temple with an axe. She, in all probability, was a mother.

Why had the ZEC, after three weeks, still not published the election results? Clearly, vote-rigging could have been a motive, but there was another. The election had, in all likelihood, given Mugabe's regime the opportunity to examine each and every ballot paper, and from them *extract the names of all those who voted against the ruling party*. This was a time-consuming process, but once the task had been completed, it would be possible for Mugabe's bloodthirsty thugs to complete the task of beating and torturing each and every one of these people.

It is sometimes forgotten that Mugabe has destroyed the lives, not only of his victims, but also of their oppressors, the torturers and persecutors – the ZANU-PF youth wing, the war veterans, the police, the army. Take the ZANU-PF youth militia. These young men have been brutalised by the Mugabe regime. They are so used to beating, maiming, and murdering that they know no other way. Not for them the opportunities which Mugabe had: of schooling, a university education, a job or profession.

On 25 April, the MDC's Harare headquarters were raided by Mugabe's riot police. Computers were seized and 250 people taken away: members of staff, and others who had sought refuge from ZANU-PF violence. Why? To disrupt the MDC's organisation, no doubt, but it was also a certainty that those computers would be examined for the names and addresses of MDC supporters, who would then be targeted. For Mugabe, retribution is the primum mobile.

The premises of the Zimbabwean Election Support Network – an independent monitoring group – were also been raided. The raid gave Mugabe the opportunity to plumb new depths of depravity. His henchmen gathered up 24 babies and 40 children under the age of six belonging to those who were seized, and imprisoned them in filthy cells in Harare.[4]

On 26 April came news at long last that must have angered Mugabe beyond measure, but delighted the MDC. So far, the ZEC had recounted votes in 18 of the 23 disputed parliamentary constituencies, and could confirm that in all of these, the original results stood. In other words, Mugabe's almost superhuman efforts to rig the parliamentary election had been in vain.

On 28 April, the two rival factions of the MDC announced that they had reunited. The following day came and went with no publication of the results of the elections which had taken place exactly one calendar month previously, neither for the remaining parliamentary seats, which were allegedly being recounted, nor the presidential poll. Why this unconscionable delay? For one, Justice George Chiweshe, Chairman of the ZEC, had a vested interest in preserving the status quo, his farm at Mazowe having been awarded to him by Mugabe's regime as part of the so-called 'Third Chimurenga', the third phase of land redistribution which commenced in 2000. During the 2001 purge, when judges unsympathetic to the regime were dismissed, Chiweshe was invited to the Bench. In his judicial decisions from that time, he would have the opportunity to express his gratitude to his master, Mugabe.

As always, the enigmatic figure of Thabo Mbeki, president of the most powerful country in the region by far, lurked in the background. As has already been mentioned, Mbeki, simply by terminating Mugabe's oil and arms supplies, could have ended Zimbabwe's woes. Moreover, he could have done this several years before, which would have entirely averted the later catastrophe. And having been appointed 'facilitator on Zimbabwe' by the other seven SADC presidents (who, with him, attended the summit meeting at Lusaka, Zambia, on 12 April) he found himself in an even stronger position to influence events. However, the weeks passed and still no election results appeared. Mbeki must bear a heavy responsibility for failing to bring Mugabe's demoniacal regime to an end.

Towards the end of May 2008, disquieting reports began to emanate from Johannesburg to the effect that there and elsewhere in South Africa, immigrants, including Zimbabwean ex-patriots, were being attacked and murdered by local people. The problem was that the immigrants, especially those from Zimbabwe whose numbers ran into millions, were swamping the labour market and competing with locals for jobs, which in that country were already hard to come by. (The unemployment rate in South Africa for unskilled workers is among the highest in the world, at about 40%.) Also, not being entitled to state benefits, the immigrants were resorting to crime in order to survive. By 22 May, the death toll had risen to 42, with 30,000 or so persons displaced from their homes and taking refuge in police stations, churches, and community centres. Mbeki should have foreseen that the destabilization of Zimbabwe by Mugabe would inevitably have a knock on effect in South Africa.

Tsvangirai was absolutely right in his assessment of Mbkei, who had no intention at that time of denouncing Mugabe. Mbeki was still firmly rooted in the past days of the liberation struggle, which for Southern Rhodesia ended more than a quarter of a century ago. He could only see Mugabe as the revolutionary and freedom fighter, and not the tyrant who has extinguished the flame of freedom in his country.

The accusatory finger can pointed at others. The presidents of the SADC and the members of the ZEC are well aware that while they continue to deliberate about Zimbabwe, Mugabe continues to kill and maim those who have dared to vote against him. Is this, then, their hope? That by drawing the proceedings out endlessly, they are giving Mugabe the time he needs totally to eliminate the opposition in Zimbabwe? This done, the inconvenient problem would then simply go away. It is a terrible possibility, but real enough.

On 29 April, MDC General Secretary Tendai Biti appealed to the UN Security Council to appoint a special envoy to be sent to Zimbabwe to help resolve the crisis. Aided by China, Russia, and Libya amongst others, South Africa chose to block Biti's appeal.

China exerts a baleful infuence in all this. In excess of 35 Chinese companies are currently operating in Zimbabwe. China is hungry for that country's minerals, and trade between the two is expected shortly to reach US$ 500 million. Writing in *The Sunday Times* on 27 April,

Michael Sheridan pointed out that although Poly Technologies – the manufacturer of the weapons aboard the ship *An Yue Jiang* which were destined for Zimbabwe – is listed as a subsidiary of the China International Investment Corporation, it is in reality:

> … a front for an elite within the country's military-industrial complex, and that it reports to the general staff department of the People's Liberation Army. Company documents show that Poly Technologies … is ultimately controlled by a clique from China's pre-eminent military clans with close ties to the Communist Party leadership and army. Major General He Ping, the company's chairman, is the son-in-law of Deng Xiaoping, the former Chinese leader; its president, Wang Jun, is the son of a vice-president and a Deng ally. Its upper ranks are stuffed with military veterans and their offspring, who have greatly enriched themselves with arms sales to some of Africa's bloodiest trouble spots.

In the abstract, it is difficult to see how, on the one hand, China could argue publicly for the establishment of democracy in Zimbabwe (even if it so wished) when this is something it continues to deny to its own people. It is, therefore, in the interests of the Chinese hierarchy that the status quo in Zimbabwe is maintained.

Torture and interrogation camps had been set up by Mugabe's regime principally in the Shona provinces of Mashonaland and Masvingo and also in Manicaland. This indicates that Mugabe sees the conflict not primarily in racial terms, for he persecutes those who oppose him whatever their ethnic background and even if they derive, as do the Shona, from the same ethnic group as himself.

On 1 May, the ZEC finally confirmed to an all-party meeting that Morgan Tsvangirai had won 47.9 per cent of the vote in March's Presidential Election; whereas Mugabe had won only 43.2 per cent. However, this was short of the 50 per cent required for outright victory. A run-off would, therefore, be required, and this must be held within three weeks. What the ZEC should have gone on to say was that, with 40 per cent of the electorate having been driven out of the country by the murderous Mugabe, there was absolutely no possibility of a free and fair election, and Tsvangirai was, therefore, the winner. Of course they did not.

In fact, there were many ways in which the ZEC could have assisted Zimbabwe. It could have declared the disenfranchisement of the 4 million or so Zimbabwean refugees (mainly living in South Africa) to be illegal, re-enfranchised them, provided facilities at which they

A boy cleans his shoes ready for school, in the midst of what remains of his home.

could vote and supervised the procedure to ensure that there was no cheating. More fundamentally than this, when the ZEC announced the results of the presidential election, it could simply have disqualified Mugabe as a candidate, on the grounds of his having grossly violated the electoral process. Finally, in the proposed run off for the presidency, the ZEC should have simply barred Mugabe from standing, as an unfit person to hold office.

The number of murdered MDC supporters and officials would soon rise to 20:

> The regime of Robert Mugabe's violent onslaught on the MDC continues without remorse. Four more members of the MDC have been killed in Guruve, seven shot in Rusape, and one died on his way to hospital.[5]

True to form, despite the fact that the free press throughout the world carried images of Zimbabwe's maimed and mutilated people, accompanied by reports from unimpeachable sources – both black and white – of the beatings and torture of the victims, so spokesmen for Mugabe's regime continued to deny that there was a problem. 'Things are quite peaceful. Things are quite normal,' said Rugare Gumbo, Agriculture Minister. 'The problem is coming from the MDC,' said

Bright Matonga, Deputy Information Minister. Zimbabwe's electoral system was 'transparent'.

Tsvangirai must now have regretted the fact that the two factions of the MDC had not reunited *before* the Presidential Election, rather than after it. Had this happened, he would have been well past the winning post on the first vote. Sadly, this was not the case, and he was now in a dilemma. If he agreed to participate in the run off, then he would be exposing his followers to another reign of pre-election terror from Mugabe's Gauleiters and thugs, which would probably continue for another month or so after the election, whilst the ZEC engaged itself in the interminable process of reckoning up the votes. But if he declined, he would forfeit the election.

With a thorough knowledge of how Mugabe has reacted in the past to those situations which are likely to affect him adversely, and with some knowledge of the workings of his mind – which will be discussed in detail shortly – it is possible to make an educated guess as to what he would do if the MDC decided to participate in a run-off with him for the presidency. The conclusions are truly terrifying.

The more the world shows its outrage, the more emboldened Mugabe becomes. Mugabe was unlikely ever to loosen his vice-like grip on power voluntarily. If there was to be a re-run of the Presidential Election, he would use every weapon in his power, if necessary expend every Chinese-made bomb, bullet, grenade and shell, to deny opposition supporters access to the polling stations. In short, Mugabe would, in all probability, visit upon the innocent and defenceless citizens of Zimbabwe a veritable holocaust of death and destruction, the like of which had not been seen since the massacres in Matabeleland by his 5th Brigade in the 1980s.

On 10 May, Morgan Tsvangirai announced that he would contest the presidential run-off, and that people would feel 'betrayed' if he failed to do so. However, he called for an end to the violence, for international monitors and for the media to be granted unrestricted access to the country; and also for a change in the composition of the ZEC.

On 14 May, the government changed the law to its own ends – something of a longstanding habit – extending the period in which the run-off election must be held for the presidency from 21 days to 90 days. The deadline was now July 31. This, of course, was designed to give Mugabe the opportunity to prolong his reign of terror and persecute all those opposition supporters with whom his thugs had not yet caught up. MDC spokesman Nelson Chamisa declared that such an act was both illegal and unfair. The MDC also pointed out that, to date, 32 of its supporters had been killed. On 16 May, the government announced that the re-run of the Presidential Election would take place on Friday 27 June – almost at the last minute. Tsvangirai announced that he was delaying his return to Zimbabwe because of concerns that there was a plot to kill him. 'We have received information from a credible source, concerning a planned assassination attempt,' said his spokesman George Sibotshiwe. This was entirely plausible. If, for all his bludgeoning, Mugabe still found himself faced with inevitable electoral defeat, then his last resort would be to murder Tsvangirai.

On 29 May 2008 the Archbishop of Canterbury Dr Rowan Williams drew attention to Mugabe's targeting of members of Zimbabwe's Anglican Church for murderous attacks, and the following day, both he and the Archbishop of Cape Town, the Most Reverend Thabo Makgoba challenged United Nations Secretary General Ban Ki-moon to intervene. As for Tsvangirai, he described Zimbabwe as 'a nation in despair'.

Senator David Coltart of the MDC shed new light on Mugabe's tactics. The violence, even by Zimbabwe's standards was unprecendented, and extended not only to the gouging out of eyes, but also to the cutting out of tongues, by Mugabe's men. This was occurring mainly in the north-east of the country, affecting between 25,000 and 50,000 people. This, said Coltart, was because certain members of ZANU-PF and the Army were not prepared to condone such activity in areas where they themselves had influence. Coltart was confident, therefore, that when the run-off election for the presidency took place, Mugabe would still be heavily defeated.

Meanwhile, Mugabe's ministers continued to pedal the same old lies – that the MDC was simply a front, which existed to facilitate a white takeover of the country, and in Zimbabwe, Mugabe's wife Grace in *The Herald* newspaper declared ominously that her husband would never hand over power to Tsvangirai.

23

Making Sense of Mugabe

Over the years, people – black and white, high and low – have struggled to make sense of Robert Gabriel Mugabe. Mugabe's former school friend David Garwe, described him as:

> … someone who kept a little apart from everyone … I don't remember him taking part in sport or school plays. He always seemed to enjoy his own company.[1]

Mugabe's brother Donato thought that 'His only friends were books.'[2] White Rhodesian Guy Clutton-Brock described Mugabe as 'a bit of a cold fish at times'.[3] British reporter Nicholas Ashwood said he was 'an ascetic figure who does not drink or smoke and smiles only rarely'.[4]

British Foreign Secretary Lord Carrington described him as 'a very formidable man, although I think rather sinister'.[5] Sir Michael Palliser, Head of the British Foreign Office, said of him, 'He had a very sharp, rather aggressive, and unpleasant manner.'[6]

South African prelate Desmond Tutu said that Mugabe had 'become increasingly insecure, he's hitting out. One just wants to weep. It's very sad'.[7] South African lawyer, statesman, and Nobel Prize winner Nelson Mandela described those African leaders who 'once commanded liberation armies and ... despise the very people who put them in power and think it's a privilege to be there for eternity ... Everybody knows well who I am talking about'.[8] Morgan Tsvangirai described Mugabe as 'a deranged despot'. In the same vein, Edgar Tekere, who once challenged Mugabe for the presidency, called him, 'an insane head of state'. Ian Smith labelled him 'the apostle of Satan'. Wilfred Mhande, a former ZANLA commander, described Mugabe as 'arrogant, paranoid, secretive and only interested in power'.[9] Said Doris Lessing, who was brought up in Southern Rhodesia and awarded the Nobel Prize for Literature in 2007, 'What's going on in Zimbabwe is a terrible story. It's

Archbishop Desmond Tutu.

a strange thing, but people who are mad in a political context ... can get away with it.'[10]

It is generally recognised that there was, and is, something terribly and tragically abnormal about Mugabe, and yet no one has managed to comprehend precisely what this abnormality is. This is because, in the main, they attempt to judge his behaviour by normal human yardsticks. What they have not realised is that, in the author's opinion, he is suffering from an intractable personality disorder – one of the features of which is that he cannot tell the difference between right and wrong.

Antisocial (or Dissocial) Personality Disorder (APD – formerly known as Psychopathic Personality Disorder) is a psychiatric condition characterised by an individual's common disregard for social rules, norms, and cultural codes, as well as impulsive behaviour, and indifference to the rights and feelings of others.[11] Here are six of its most common characteristics:

When Mugabe came to power in 1980, Nelson Mandela still had ten more years of imprisonment to endure.

1. Callous unconcern for the feelings of others.

Mugabe is unperturbed by the fact that, under his regime, an estimated 3–6 million people have been murdered or have died from starvation, neglect, or the effects of untreated Aids.

In the days of the Smith regime, Judith Todd, daughter of Sir Garfield Todd, former Prime Minister of Rhodesia, suffered imprisonment on account of her efforts to promote full, black enfranchisement. Under the Mugabe regime, she would be abused in a quite different way. When, in February 1983, she complained to two of Mugabe's senior army officers that the 5th Brigade was massacring civilians in Matabeleland, one of them subsequently punished her by raping her at gun-point.[12] It will be remembered that Mugabe's very first teaching post was with Judith's father, RS Garfield Todd. He, like her, had always supported the black cause, and both had been imprisoned on this account in 1972 by the white regime. This violation, undoubtedly performed with the full connivance of Mugabe, was a betrayal of the most chilling and sinister kind.

2. Gross and persistent attitude of irresponsibility and disregard for social norms, rules, and obligations.

Mugabe's irresponsible and self-seeking behaviour has led to an inflation rate in excess of 100,000 per cent, and a virtual halving of life expectancy for the population. It might be imagined that a government faced with widespread starvation in its country would encourage food production from whatever source. Not so in Zimbabwe, where on 5 October 2007, ten white farmers appeared in court accused of growing crops on their land in the Chegutu District, 70 miles south-west of Harare. They were charged with violating the Consequential Provisions Act, which gave the few hundred white farmers who remained a final deadline of 30 September 2007 to vacate their farms and their homes.[13]

Mugabe has a degree in law, and yet he disdains the rule of law:

> The courts can do whatever they want, but no judicial decision will stand in our way ... My own position is that we should not even be defending our position in the courts.[14]

His reaction, if the law does not suit his purpose, is to hound the judges out of office and change the law to suit himself. When his ZANU-PF thugs break the law by their murderous activities, he is quick to grant them immunity.

He has a similar disdain for democracy, vote rigging being one speciality, as has been amply demonstrated, and intimidation another.

3. Incapacity to maintain enduring relationships.

Mugabe has innumerable henchmen and lackeys to do his will, but he appears to have few, if any, close friends.

4. Very low tolerance of frustration and low threshold for discharge of aggression, including violence.

Mugabe cannot bear the slightest opposition or criticism, and is apt to flare up suddenly and at any moment in an uncontrollable temper, exacting an instant and often bloody revenge on those who stand in his way, black or white.

When he married his second wife Grace, he anticipated that she, being an heiress, would bring with her a considerable dowry. When her family refused to countenance such an idea, Mugabe angrily smashed every window in his official residence, Government House.[15]

His behaviour may be likened to that of a spoilt child. But whereas most children mature and 'grow out' of such antisocial tendencies, with Mugabe they have persisted. Even his language is infantile — 'The police … have the right to bash them.'

5. Incapacity to experience guilt or to profit from experience.

Mugabe has never expressed the slightest remorse for anything he has done. His degree in Economics appears to have profited him little. His history degree in History afforded him no insights into political change. He learned nothing from the experience and advice of his neighbours Machel, Kaunda, and Banda, all of whom urged him, when he came to power, to harness the expertise of the whites and work with them for the benefit of the country.

6. Marked proneness to blame others, or to offer plausible rationalisations for the behaviour that has brought the subject into conflict with society.

Mugabe constantly vilifies the West, and in particular Britain, whom he blames for all Zimbabwe's ills. This is to ignore the fact that even prior to Smith's Unilateral Declaration of Independence, Britain was in favour of black majority rule. The British are 'bad' by definition. There is no recognition – let alone gratitude – for the aid (in excess of £0.5 billion to date) that the British government has provided for Zimbabwe since independence. Nor is any thanks given to the individual citizens of Britain, who have donated generously to the charitable organisations operating in Zimbabwe. Britain is also accused of plotting to re-colonise the country.

The cause of Antisocial Personality Disorder is unknown, though both genetic and environmental factors may play a part. It is a lifelong condition, and it alters little with the passing of time.[16]

24

Epilogue

On 31 May 2008, Zimbabwe army Chief-of-Staff Major General Martin Chedondo told his soldiers, 'If you have other thoughts [than of voting for Mugabe] then you should remove the uniform.' This he argued was because when they had joined the armed forces, they had promised to protect Mugabe as the defender of the revolution. Thus Chedondo demonstrated his contempt for the principles of democracy.

Absurd and obscene as it may seem, on 3 June 2008, Mugabe addressed a summit meeting in Rome hosted by the United Nations Food and Agriculture Organisation, whose aim is to combat hunger and poverty and to boost agricultural production. How ironic, because that very day, the relief agency Care International was ordered to cease operations in Harare, thus condemning thousands more Zimbabweans to starvation – the excuse being that aid agencies were, according to Mugabe, 'using food as a political weapon with which to campaign against the government'. Meanwhile, as his henchmen back at home were busy starving and murdering their political opponents – the death toll amongst MDC supporters having now risen to 65 – Mugabe and his aides, including chefs and waiters he had brought with him, enjoyed the hospitality of the five-star Ambassadorial Palace Hotel.

In attending the summit, Mugabe had been able to avoid the travel ban placed on him six years earlier by the EU because the conference was held under the auspices of the UN. (Evidence enough, surely, that the UN is in urgent need of reform.) In his speech, Mugabe waxed lyrical about his achievements, declaring: 'Over the past decade, Zimbabwe has democratised land ownership.' Regrettably, however, this had:

> … elicited wrath from our former colonial master. In retaliation for the measures we took to empower the black majority, the United Kingdom has mobilised its friends in Europe, North America, Australia and New Zealand to impose economic sanctions against Zimbabwe.

As usual, this was a lie, in that the only sanctions were the travel ban and the freezing of Mugabe's assets and those of his Zanu-PF officials. The EU had an arms embargo, not the UN. Mugabe also failed to mention that the UK's Department for International Development was due to spend about £40 million in the coming year on aid for Zimbabwe.

On 4 June 2008, the Mugabe regime cocked another snook at world opinion by interrupting Tsvangirai and his entourage as they campaigned for the forthcoming Presidential Election. The MDC leader was held for four hours at the roadside and for another four hours in a police station before being released without charge.

On 5 June, Zimbabwean police detained a group of US and UK diplomats as they were travelling about the country investigating political violence. The following day, the work of all aid groups and non-governmental organisations in Zimbabwe was suspended indefinitely, Social Welfare Minister Nicholas Goche accusing them of 'breaching the terms of their registration.' This included the Save the Children fund. Western media reporters declared, understating the case somewhat, that this action 'would have a significant impact', and that conditions in the country would 'deteriorate significantly'. What they meant was that millions were now facing an imminent threat of death by starvation.

On Friday 6, Tsvangirai was forced to suspend campaigning after being detained for a second time, this time at Esigodini police station in the south. 'They told us we cannot hold rallies. They said Morgan Tsvangirai should not even hold those walkabouts as they would attract crowds,' said MDC Chairman Lovemore Moyo.

Reports emanating from Zimbabwe revealed exactly how Mugabe's plan of flushing out the opposition supporters by using food as a weapon was intended to work. In the absence of aid agencies and NGOs, it was the Government which now controlled the food supplies. What happened in practice was this. A starving Zimbabwean goes to the village headman to beg for food – and it is estimated that at least 2 million people in the country were and are dependent on food aid. If that person held a ZANU-PF Party card, then his request was likely to be granted. If he was an MDC supporter who refused to change his mind and promise to vote for Mugabe, his request for food was denied, and his identity card confiscated, in order to make it

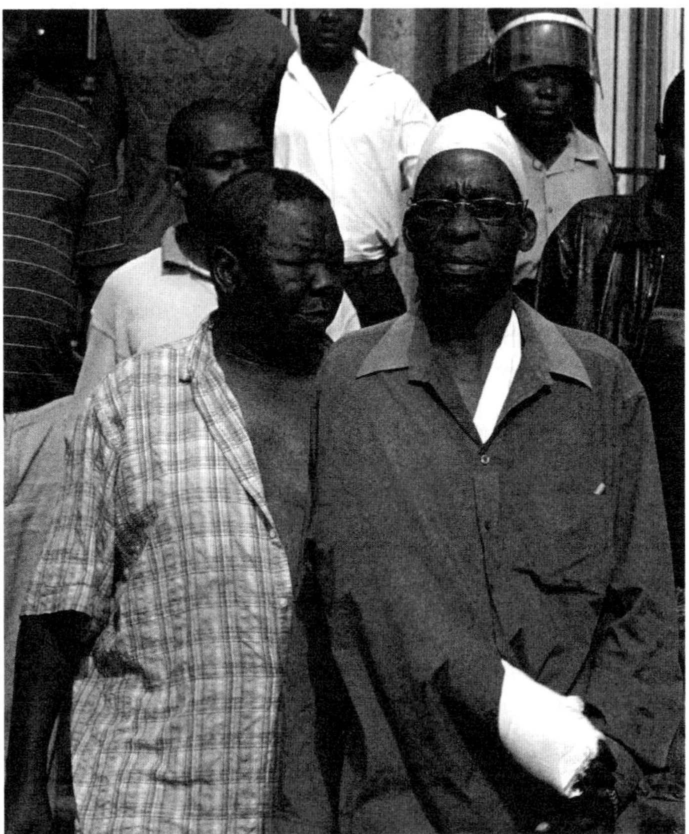

Tsvangirai with constitutional lawyer Lovemore Madhuku.

impossible for him to vote in the forthcoming Presidential Election. Now that this person had been identified as an opponent of Mugabe, the ZANU-PF Youth Militia was alerted. The young men were plied with drink and drugs, told that the MDC was involved in a plot with Britain to take over the country, and dispatched to that Zimbabwean's home to beat, torture, or even murder him or her.

It is desperately disappointing that, since the foundation of the League of Nations in 1919 – which became the United Nations in 1945 – no mechanism exists for the removal of gangster regimes run by fiendishly cruel and tyrannical figures such as Mugabe. (Zimbabwe, of course, is not the only 'rogue state' in which such a state of affairs exists.)

On 7 June 2008, the Zimbabwean High Court overturned the ban imposed by the police on political rallies. However, previous rulings by the court had been ignored, lending weight to the view expressed by US Ambassador to Zimbabwe James McGee that:

> Zimbabwe is now a lawless country. They are not following their own laws. They are not following International law.

On 9 June, Nobel Peace Prize Laureate Archbishop Desmond Tutu, who was on a visit to Britain, spoke at a service for peace held at London's Church of St Martin in the Fields. Of the current situation in Zimbabwe, he said: 'It is a dream, that has turned into the most horrendous nightmare, and we say "for goodness sake, Mr President, you have been president for 20 years. That is enough. How about standing down."'

On 10 June, Tsvangirai declared that Zimbabwe was, in effect, being run by a military junta. To that date, 66 opposition supporters had been killed in the political violence since the disputed elections in March, and another 200 were unaccounted for.

The suspicion that the military was actively involved in running Mugabe's election campaign was confirmed by information contained in two documents given to BBC Correspondent Ian Pannell. The documents described how senior figures in ZANU-PF, its main committee, and the Joint Operations Command (JOC, composed of military and police chiefs) were managing the campaign for the forthcoming election. They described in detail how the campaign was to be conducted, with the use of food as a political weapon, the mobilisation of war veterans, the harassing of the opposition's political activists, the driving of opposition supporters from their homes, and covert operations intended 'to decompose the [MDC] opposition.'

As the date for the election approached, Mugabe became increasingly uninhibited in his use of terrorism. His ZANU-PF Youth Militia were now given carte blanche to move into the suburbs of the capital Harare itself and abduct its residents, not under cover of darkness, but in broad daylight; not to take them to some remote place of torture out in the bush, but to axe, beat, rape, and burn alive Mugabe's political opponents on the spot.

For the first time, in all the long years since Mugabe began to commit atrocities against his people, a substantial number – forty in all – of Africa's most prominent figures rallied together to criticise him, by publishing an open letter calling on the violence to cease. Signatories to this letter were Kofi Annan, Desmond Tutu, and several former national leaders, including Jerry Rawlings of Ghana, Joaquim Chissano of Mozambique, and Abdulsalami Alhaji Abubakar of Nigeria. In addition, on 13 June, Phandu Sekelema, Foreign Minister of Botswana, declared that the repeated arrests of members of the opposition 'do not auger well for a free, fair, and democratic election. People must be free to campaign'.

Tsvangirai himself had been arrested no less than four times in the previous eight days, and having spent the night of 12/13 June in a police cell, he was released only to find that his two campaign buses had been impounded.

Just in case it should be thought that China is the only country to have supported Zimbabwe, it was revealed by reporter Maurice Gerard writing in *The Daily Telegraph* on 14 June that the Zimbabwean subsidiary of the UK's Barclays Bank:

> ... lent the Mugabe regime $46.4 million (£23 million) last year through its purchase of government and municipal bonds, and is one of the main contributors to a government-run loan scheme for farm improvements.

Laudable as this may sound, Gerard then revealed that 'At least five [government] ministers have received loans for farms seized from white Zimbabweans.' This is despite the fact that sanctions imposed on Zimbabwe by the EU in 2002 'prohibit any British bank from giving financial services to individuals connected with the government'.

On 18 June, the Zimbabwean Broadcasting Corporation announced that it would no longer carry the opposition's party political broadcasts on its radio station. The same conditions already applied to those newspapers controlled by ZANU-PF.

On 19 June, the MDC reported that the bodies of four youths, who had been severely tortured, had been discovered near Harare, bringing the total number of opposition supporters known to have been killed to 70. (Two of these victims were, in fact, killed before the very eyes of independent election monitors.) The blindfolded body of Abigail, the 27-year-old wife of Harare's mayor, MDC Councillor Emmanuel Chiroto (who had been elected mayor only four days previously), was found in a forest close to her burnt-out home.

Meanwhile, the voices of protest became a swelling chorus of condemnation, as Tanzania's Foreign Minister Bernard Membe stated that 'There is every sign that these elections will never be free or fair.' (Tanzania being the current chair of the African Union.) Membe said that he and the Foreign Ministers of Swaziland and Angola would write to their presidents, 'so that they do something urgently so that we can save Zimbabwe.' The Presidents of Ruanda, Senegal, and Zambia added their voice to the chorus of condemnation.

In this apocalyptic nightmare, Morgan Tsvangirai still conducted himself in a dignified way, even when complaining about how the hours he had spent in detention at various police stations had prevented him from pursuing the election trail in his long red bus, emblazoned with his portrait and the words 'MORGAN IS THE ONE'.

The external protests grew ever louder. United Nations Secretary-General Ban Ki-moon told the UN General Assembly in New York that he was profoundly alarmed and that 'Violence, intimidation, and the arrest of opposition leaders are not conducive to credible elections.' The UN, he said, was prepared to provide monitors for the forthcoming election. Kenyan Prime Minister Raila Odinga, at a news conference attended by US Secretary of State Condoleezza Rice, said that Mugabe had made a 'sham' of the presidential election, and called for a UN peacekeeping force to be put in place in the country. Marwick Khumalo, head of the 64-member Pan-African Parliament observer mission said that he would not endorse the vote if the violence continued. SADC official Tanki Mothae said that he had received reports from various parts of the country about houses being torched, abductions, and the discovery of corpses.

Thabo Mbeki met with representatives of the government and the opposition, but as usual, had little to say about the outcome. President of South Africa's ANC, Jacob Zuma, however, said 'I think we will be lucky if we have free and fair elections, but we hope for that.'

In a remarkable volte-face, one of Mugabe's staunchest allies, Angolan President Jose Eduardo dos Santos (whose country had already previously refused permission for the Chinese ship *An Yue Jiang* carrying arms to Zimbabwe to use its ports to unload its cargo) sent a letter to him urging him to 'observe the spirit of tolerance, respect for difference, and cease all forms of intimidation and political violence.' Santos's words inevitably fell on deaf ears: 'Only God who appointed me will remove me, not the MDC, not the British.'

On 22 June, ZANU-PF Youth Militia surrounded Harare's Glamis Stadium, where Tsvangirai had planned to hold a key election rally, and using sticks and iron bars they beat MDC supporters and also those journalists who were present. Whereupon Tsvangirai made the following announcement:

> We in the MDC have resolved that we will no longer participate in this violent, illegitimate sham of an election process. Conditions as of today do not permit the holding of a credible poll. We cannot ask the people to cast their vote on June 27 when that vote will cost their lives.

This meant that Mugabe would automatically become the President of Zimbabwe for another 'term'. To that date, human rights groups estimated that 85 opposition supporters had been killed, and 30,000 or more driven from their homes.

On 23 June, the 15-member UN Security Council unanimously - if belatedly – condemned the violence perpetrated against the opposition in Zimbabwe, and declared that a free and fair election on June 27 would be 'impossible'.

On the same day, Tsvangirai, who feared for his life, took refuge in the Dutch Embassy in Harare. The international clamour against Mugabe increased, as the Zimbabwean leader announced that the Presidential Election would go ahead on Friday 27 June, come what may. 'The Mugabe regime has no electoral legitimacy to claim the mantle of government' – Stephen Smith, Foreign Minister of Australia. 'The forthcoming election was 'a travesty of democracy' – Javier Solana, EU Foreign Policy supremo Mugabe was nothing more than 'a crook and a mass murderer' – French Foreign Minister Bernard Kouchner. The US declared that it would not recognise the outcome Presidential Election. And the criticism also came from inside Africa. Mugabe was 'thumbing his nose at the International Community' – Desmond Tutu. It was 'scandalous for SADC to remain silent on Zimbabwe' – President Mwanawasa of Zambia. Senegalese President Abdoulaye Wade advocated the establishment of a transitional government, arranged through Mbeki and the SADC, with Tsvangirai as prime minister, but stopped short of saying what Mugabe's role was to be in this.

With election day fast approaching, Moeletsi Mbeki, Deputy Director of the South African Institute of International Affairs, was able to explain, in an interview for the BBC, South Africa's stubborn and steadfast support of the Mugabe regime:

> I think South Africa will continue supporting the Mugabe Government, and I think all the other African countries will do so ... The great majority of the people of South Africa are strongly opposed to what Mugabe is doing, but our government is sympathetic ... I think because the current government has the common enemy of the trade unions, who are against it in South Africa, and the trade unions are against the Mugabe regime, so

> they have a common enemy. And so, on the principle that my enemy's enemy is my friend, I think this is why my government feels sympathetic to the Mugabe regime.

In other words, Thabo Mbeki's attitude is motivated by a fear that if the Mugabe regime falls, than this will encourage the trade unions in South Africa to become more assertive, and perhaps threaten his regime also.

As members of the ZEC prepared – for reasons best known to themselves – to monitor the re-run of the Presidential Election, which, needless to say, would be even more of a farce than the original one, so the authoritative voice of Nelson Mandela reverberated around the world, as he referred to 'the tragic failure of leadership in our neighbour, Zimbabwe.' (18 July would be Mandela's 90th birthday.)

The SADC, going further than it had gone before, urged Mugabe to postpone the election on the grounds that it was now illegitimate. It expressed disappointment that Tsvangirai had withdrawn from the race, before making the absurd comment that 'the people of Zimbabwe can solve their own problems.'

On the advice of Foreign Secretary David Miliband, HM The Queen stripped Mugabe of his honorary knighthood, (conferred on him in 1994), as a 'mark of revulsion' at human rights abuses, citing Mugabe's 'abject disregard' for democracy. Losing the honour, Mugabe joined a very exclusive club indeed, its only other member of recent times being the Romanian dictator Nicolae Ceausescu.

Election day arrived and small groups of electors queued in line at the polling booths, watched by SADC monitors attired in black, and wearing red baseball caps. Inside the booths, the ballot papers were scrutinised, and those who had voted for Mugabe presented their little fingers – which were dyed with indelible red ink – as a sign of approval. Those who failed to vote in the 'correct' manner, or who simply decided not to participate in the poll were now easily identifiable. They could be hunted down by Mugabe's thugs, to be beaten, starved, and perhaps murdered. BBC World Affairs editor John Simpson declared, as an eye-witness, that the scene was reminiscent of Nazi Germany, with Mugabe's sinister-looking militia, armed with batons and toting guns, watching menacingly over everything and everybody. Was there ever a greater travesty of an election than this?

Mugabe himself, attired in light-brown suit, white shirt and pink tie, cast his vote exuberantly; although he did fail to insert his ballot paper into the slot in the ballot box on his first attempt – to the amusement of his watching wife and henchmen.

In contrast to the previous election, the result was declared within 24 hours of the poll booths closing, and election officials declared that Mugabe, in a landslide victory, had won in all ten provinces with 85.5% of the vote. Within minutes, Mugabe was inaugurated as President for another five-year term. 'I do swear that I will well and truly serve Zimbabwe,' he said, in front of an audience who had of course been invited to the ceremony well before the results were announced. Meanwhile, the MDC declared that the death toll amongst its supporters had risen to 90; that 10,000 had been injured; 10,000 homes burned, and 200,000 persons displaced.

One of the few people who had grasped, or who was prepared to admit, exactly what Mugabe was about was Philip Chikwiramakomo, of the charity WeZimbabwe:

> For me, as a Zimbabwean, I could almost literally see blood dripping out of Mugabe's hands onto the Bible. It was incredibly ironic for him to be saying to the rest of the world that he solemnly swears to serve Zimbabwe, when in his 28 years in power, all he has served well has been a cocktail of disaster, violence, and oppression.

When asked about the future, Chikwiramakomo had no words of comfort to offer:

> There is the retribution. It cannot be said enough. Mugabe goes for total elimination. He did it in the 1980s with Joshua Nkomo and ZAPU, and he will try to eliminate the MDC and ensure thay are incapable of operating in Zimbabwe. The violence will go on for some time yet.

A terrible danger now has to be faced, and there will be many who will simply not believe it, and who will try to convince themselves that nobody could be that evil. However, it is by examining and understanding the past, that an informed and intelligent guess may be made as to what the future holds.

The psychological assessment of Mugabe presented in chapter 23 shows him to be someone lacking in both humanity and compassion. From his perspective, he has seen the UN to be divided, and the AU to be little more than a talking shop. He attended the African Union summit on Monday June 30 at Sharm-El-Sheikh, Egypt, straight after his 'victory', confident that there would be little direct condemnation from any of the 53 countries represented. Also, he knows that the EU and the US are unlikely to intervene for fear of being branded imperialist.

He can therefore act with impunity. Furthermore, he has banned aid workers, and after the so-called presidential election on June 27 the electoral monitors will all have gone home. All he then has to do is to expel all foreign journalists from the country and there will be no witnesses available to tell the outside world about what is to follow. And what is to follow?

'How can a ballpoint fight with a gun?' asked Mugabe, surely knowingly giving the lie to Edward Bulwer-Lytton's assertion, made in 1839, that 'The pen is mightier than the sword.' This is entirely in accordance with Mugabe's long held belief that might is right. It is yet another indication of what he is prepared to do in order to silence those who dare to criticise him. Indeed, the indications are, from the recent behaviour of ZANU-PF's Youth Wing (which Mugabe has unashamedly modelled on the Hitler Youth) that a bloodbath on a massive scale is about to begin.

To satisfy his seemingly insatiable appetite for revenge against those who have dared to speak against him, it is the author's belief that Mugabe will now embark on a campaign of unrestrained terror, torture, and mass murder as has not been seen in Southern Africa for over a hundred years.

The tragedy of Zimbabwe has not come to an end. Any book will always be out-of-date when published, by its very nature. The last words should belong to the author of that tragedy. They bring to mind George Orwell's vision in *1984*: 'If you want a picture of the future, imagine a boot stamping on a human face – forever.'

Mugabe declared that it was whilst he was in Ghana that he decided to become a Marxist. However, when Ian Smith asked him how he could support a failed system like communism, Mugabe, uncharacteristically allowing his guard to drop for a moment, replied:

> It has nothing to do with the philosophy of communism, which is foreign to us black people. What appealed to us most over our induction into communism was the firm instruction that: 'Once you had become the government, you remain in government for ever.'

Notes

Chapter 1: Education

[1] Meredith, Martin. *Mugabe: Power and Plunder in Zimbabwe*, p.19.
[2] Ibid, p.21.
[3] Williams, Basil. 1921. *Cecil Rhodes*. London: Constable, p.381.
[4] Blair, David. *Degrees in Violence*, p.18.
[5] Ibid, p.19.
[6] Blake, Robert. *History of Rhodesia*, p.374.
[7] Meredith, op.cit., p.24.

Chapter 3: On a Collision Course: Black Nationalism and White Procrastination

[1] Macmillan, Harold. Speech to South African Houses of Parliament, Cape Town, 3 February 1960.
[2] Welensky, Sir Roy. *Welensky's 4,000 Days: The Life and Death of the Federation of Rhodesia and Nyasaland*, p.21.
[3] Ibid, pp.21–2.
[4] Ibid, p.23.
[5] Ibid, p.28.
[6] Ibid, p.37.
[7] Ibid, pp.38–9
[8] Ibid, p.50.
[9] Ibid, p.52.
[10] Ibid, p.16.
[11] Ibid, p.110.

Chapter 4: Nyasaland: The Fuse is Lit – Mugabe Returns Home

[1] Welensky, Sir Roy. *Welensky's 4,000 Days: The Life and Death of the Federation of Rhodesia and Nyasaland*, pp.100, 102.
[2] Ibid, pp.134, 136.
[3] Ibid, pp.109–10.
[4] Ibid, pp.127, 131.
[5] Ibid, p.131.
[6] Meredith, Martin. *Mugabe: Power and Plunder in Zimbabwe,* p.26.

Chapter 5: Mugabe the Publicist

[1] Meredith, Martin. *Mugabe: Power and Plunder in Zimbabwe,* p.27.
[2] 1961 Constitution.
[3] Smith, Ian Douglas. *Bitter Harvest: The Great Betrayal*, p.41.
[4] Meredith, op.cit., pp.28,29.
[5] Ibid, p.31.
[6] Blake, Robert. *History of Rhodesia*, pp.247–251.

Chapter 6: Mugabe is Imprisoned: The Demise of the Federation

[1] Welensky, Sir Roy. *Welensky's 4,000 Days: The Life and Death of the Federation of Rhodesia and Nyasaland*, pp.363–64.
[2] Ibid, p.365.
[3] Paul, Richard. *Kaunda: Founder of Zambia*, p.82.
[4] Healey, Denis, *The Time of My Life*, p.332.
[5] Smith, David, and C Simpson, with Ian Davies. *Mugabe*, p.56.
[6] Meredith, Martin. *Mugabe: Power and Plunder in Zimbabwe*, p.36.
[7] Royle, Trevor. *Winds of Change: The End of Empire in Africa*, p.251.

Chapter 7: Freedom and Exile

[1] *The Rhodesia Herald*, 27 January 1976.
[2] Royle, Trevor. *Winds of Change: The End of Empire in Africa*, p.259.
[3] *The Observer*, 10 October 1976.
[4] Smith, David, and C Simpson, with Ian Davies. *Mugabe*, p.95.
[5] *The Rhodesia Herald*, 17 March 1977.
[6] Smith, David, op.cit., p.101.
[7] Ibid, p.113.
[8] Ibid, p.119.

Chapter 8: The Lancaster House Conference and Beyond

[1] Smith, David, and C Simpson, with Ian Davies. *Mugabe*, p.130.
[2] Smith, Ian Douglas. *Bitter Harvest: The Great Betrayal*, p.316.

Chapter 9: Independence; Doubts About Mugabe

[1] Smith, Ian Douglas. *Bitter Harvest: The Great Betrayal* , p.336.
[2] Meredith, Martin. *Mugabe: Power and Plunder in Zimbabwe*, p.15.
[3] Smith, David, and C Simpson, with Ian Davies. *Mugabe*, p.213.
[4] Ibid, p.210.
[5] Meredith, op.cit., p.39.
[6] Ibid, p.14.
[7] Blair, David. *Degrees in Violence*, p.16.
[8] Smith, Ian Douglas, op. cit., p.342.
[9] Blair, op. cit., p.133.
[10] Smith, Ian Douglas, op. cit., p.371.
[11] Mugabe to David Coltart, 19 August 1981.
[12] Meredith, op.cit., p.52.
[13] Ibid, p.52.
[14] Blair, op.cit., p.29.
[15] Meredith, op.cit., p.86.
[16] Ibid, p.96.
[17] Ibid, p.105.

Chapter 10: Morgan Tsvangirai and The Movement for Democratic Change

[1] Meredith, Martin. *Mugabe: Power and Plunder in Zimbabwe*, p.165.
[2] Mugabe, speech during the 2000 election campaign.
[3] Thornycroft, Peta. *The Daily Telegraph*, 6 March 2002.
[4] Johnson, RW and Jacqui Goddard. *The Sunday Times*, 10 March 2002.
[5] Thornycroft, Peta. *The Daily Telegraph*, 6 March 2002.
[6] *The Daily Telegraph*, 31 July 2002.
[7] www.africaonline.com/site/Articles/1,3,50637.jsp
[8] Mapenzauswa, Stella. *The Independent*, 7 January 2003.
[9] *The Economist*, 2 March 2002.
[10] Lamb, Christina. *The Sunday Times*, 11 June 2006.
[11] Thornycroft, Peta. *The Daily Telegraph*, 15 March 2007.
[12] Connery, Neil. *The Daily Mail*, 21 September 2007.
[13] *The Daily Telegraph*, 7 April 2007.
[14] *The Daily Telegraph*, 16 March 2007.

Chapter 11: Mugabe's Loathing of the White Farmers

[1] Goodall, Elizabeth, CK Cooke and J Desmond Clark. *Prehistoric Rock Art of the Federation of Rhodesia and Nyasaland*, p.165.
[2] Rosenthal, Eric. *Encyclopedia of Southern Africa*, pp.39,63.
[3] Welensky, Sir Roy. *Welensky's 4,000 Days: The Life and Death of the Federation of Rhodesia and Nyasaland*, pp.21–2.
[4] Gale, WD. *One Man's Vision: The Story of Rhodesia*, p.171.

[5] Thomas, Antony. *Rhodes: The Race for Africa*, p.350.
[6] Vindex, FV. *Cecil Rhodes: His Political Life and Speeches*, p.386.
[7] Thomas, op.cit., p.279.
[8] Williams, Basil. 1921. *Cecil Rhodes*. London: Constable, p.381.
[9] Vindex, op.cit., pp.372,390.
[10] Pre-Independence Legislation on Land, www.raceandhistory.com/Zimbabwe/factsheet.html
[11] Ibid.
[12] Smith, David, and C Simpson, with Ian Davies. *Mugabe*, p.168.

Chapter 12: Farm Appropriation: Famine

[1] House, Margaret, John House, and Beryl Salt. *Zimbabwe: A Handbook*, p.69.
[2] Da Silva, Vicky. *The Land Issue in Zimbabwe*.
[3] Meredith, Martin. *Mugabe: Power and Plunder in Zimbabwe*, p.126.
[4] *The Economist*, 6 May 2000.
[5] *The Guardian Unlimited*
[6] Raath, Jan. *The Times*, 14 December 2002.

Chapter 13: Racism, Homophobia, Genocide

[1] Meredith, Martin. *Mugabe: Power and Plunder in Zimbabwe*, pp.9–10.
[2] Mugabe in BBC interview with David Dimbleby, 26 June 2000.
[3] Meredith, op.cit., p.203.
[4] Coughlin, Con. Bulawayo, *The Daily Mail*, 18 June 2005.
[5] Mugabe, speech, 11 November 2005.
[6] Mugabe, speech to United Nations, September 2005.
[7] Mugabe, 10 November 2005.
[8] Meredith, op.cit., p.131.
[9] University of Cincinnati, Study of Prejudicial Attitudes of White Males. *Jet* magazine, 10 January 1994.
[10] Johnson, RW. *The Sunday Times*, 7 January 2007.
[11] Mugabe, speech given at the funeral of Dr Swithin Mombeshora, March 2003.

Chapter 14: Mugabe's 'Jewel of Africa': Economic Meltdown and Social Disintegration!

[1] Butcher, Tim. *The Daily Telegraph*, 24 August 2002.
[2] Conway, Edmund. *The Daily Telegraph*, 29 May 2007.
[3] *The Economist*, 7 July 2007.
[4] *The Daily Mail*, Mail Foreign Service, 9 July 2007.
[5] Coughlin, Con. *The Daily Mail*, 18 June 2005.
[6] Dziva, Byron. *The Daily Telegraph*, 9 July 2007.
[7] St John, Lauren. *The Daily Mail*, 25 August 2007.
[8] Johnson, RW. *The Sunday Times*, 7 January 2007.

[9] *The Economist*, 23 June 2007.
[10] Spencer, Richard. *The Sunday Telegraph*, 31 August 2007.

Chapter 15: 'Nhamodzenyika' – The Suffering Country

[1] From the Old Testament, Book of Joshua.
[2] www.guineafowlschool.org (this letter subsequently removed from the website).
[3] Mellody, Michael. E-mail to Dr Andrew Norman.
[4] Blair, David. *Degrees in Violence*, p.9.
[5] Boynton, Graham. *The Sunday Telegraph*, 23 September 2007.
[6] Bevan, Stephen. *The Sunday Telegraph*, 23 September 2007.
[7] Bevan, Stephen. *The Sunday Telegraph*, 7 October 2007.

Chapter 16: Self Aggrandisement: The Winner Takes All

[1] Meredith, Martin. *Mugabe: Power and Plunder in Zimbabwe*, p.80.
[2] Ibid, p.137.
[3] Swain, Jon. *The Sunday Times*, 24 March 2002.
[4] Ibid.
[5] Webster, Philip, Adam Sage, and Rory Watson. *The Times*, 24 January 2003.
[6] BBC News.
[7] Basildon, Peta. *The Independent*, 7 April 2008.
[8] Lamb, Christina. *The Sunday Times*, 2 March 2008.
[9] Bevan, Stephen, and Michael Gwaridzo. *The Sunday Telegraph*, 20 May 2007.

Chapter 17: Lisbon: the Europe/Africa Summit

[1] Blair, David. *The Daily Telegraph*. 20 November 2007.
[2] Blair, David. *The Sunday Telegraph*. 9 December 2007.
[3] Blair, David. *The Daily Telegraph*. 10 December 2007.

Chapter 18: An Election is Called

[1] Obisesan, Aderogba. *Mail & Guardian online*. 28 February 2008.
[2] Dziva, Byron. *The Daily Telegraph*. 13 February 2008.
[3] Thornycroft, Peta. *The Daily Telegraph*. 14 February 2008.
[4] Ibid.
[5] Ibid.
[6] The Editor, *africannews.com,* 22 February 2008, and Lebo Nkatazo, *newzimbabwe.com,* 22 February 2008.
[7] *zimbabwestuation.com* 26 February 2008.
[8] Berger, Sebastien. *The Daily Telegraph*. 25 February 2008.
[9] *International Herald Tribune: The Associated Press*. 22 February 2008.
[10] Berger, Sebastien. *The Daily Telegraph*. 25 February 2008.
[11] Nkatazo, Lebo. *newsdesk newzimbabwe.com*, 22 February 2008.
[12] Bevan, Stephen. *The Sunday Telegraph*, 2 December 2007.

Chapter 19: Intimidation, Dirty Tricks, Propaganda

[1] Dziva, Byron. *The Daily Telegraph*, 13 February 2008.
[2] Nyambosi, Ngirazi *Nyasa Times*, Malawi, 25 February 2008.
[3] *The Daily Telegraph*, 6 March 2008.
[4] Raath, Jan, *The Times*. 10 March 2008.
[5] Raath, Jan, *The Times*. 27 March 2008.
[6] *The Times*. Agence France-Presse, 26 March 2008.
[7] Basildon, Peta. *The Independent*. 10 March 2008.

Chapter 20: The March 2008 Election: Further Skullduggery

[1] Raath, Jan, *The Times*. 28 March 2008.
[2] Thornycroft, Peta. *The Daily Telegraph*, 31 March 2008.
[3] *The Zimbabwean*. 'Election violence increases', 25 February 2008.
[4] Thornycroft, Peta and Sebastien Berger. *The Daily Telegraph*, 29 March 2008.
[5] Lamb, Christina. *The Sunday Times*, 30 March 2008,
[6] Raath, Jan. *The Times*, 18 March 2008.
[7] Philip, Catherine and Jonathan Clayton, *The Times*, 2 April 2008.
[8] Berger, Sebastien. *The Daily Telegraph*, 9 April 2008.
[9] Blair, David. *The Daily Telegraph*, 8 April 2008.

Chapter 21: Zimbabwe in the World Spotlight

[1] Pambazuka: Weekly Forum for Social Justice in Africa. 1 May 2008.
[2] www.guardian.co.uk, 18 April 2008.
[3] BBC News, 21 April 2008

Chapter 22: Zimbabwe's Agony Continues

[1] Luke, 18:16.
[2] Thornycroft, Peta. *The Daily Telegraph*, 24 April 2008.
[3] Genesis, 20:12.
[4] Lamb, Christina, and John Makura, *The Sunday Times*, 27 April 2008.
[5] Pambazuka: Weekly Forum for Social Justice in Africa. 1 May 2008.

Chapter 23: Making Sense of Mugabe

[1] Meredith, Martin. *Mugabe: Power and Plunder in Zimbabwe*, p.21 (quoted in David Smith and Colin Simpson, 1981, *Mugabe*. London: Sphere, 1981, p.14.)
[2] Meredith, op.cit., p.21.
[3] Ibid, p.23.
[4] *The Times*, 5 March 1980.
[5] Blair, David. *Degrees in Violence*, p.25.
[6] Meredith, op.cit., p.7.

[7] *The Dispatch*, 5 April 2000.

[8] Nelson Mandela, speaking at the launch of UNICEF Global Partnership, Johannesburg, 6 May 2000.

[9] Wilfred Mhande, interview with the Helen Suzman Foundation, December 2000.

[10] Lessing, Doris at the Edinburgh Book Festival, August 2002.

[11] World Health Organisation, ICD-10 F60.2.

[12] Berger, Sebastien, *The Daily Telegraph*, 9 July 2007, and Judith Todd, *Through the Darkness*, pp. 50–51.

[13] Thornycroft, Peta. *The Sunday Telegraph*, 6 October 2007.

[14] Meredith, op.cit., p.203.

[15] Information supplied by a former employee of Mugabe's who, for that person's own safety, must remain anonymous.

[16] Gelder, Michael, Paul Harrison, and Philip Cowen. *Shorter Oxford Textbook of Psychiatry*, p.144.

Bibliography

Blair, David. 2002. *Degrees in Violence.* London: Continuum.

Blake, Robert. 1978. *History of Rhodesia.* London: Eyre Methuen.

Boggie, Jeannie M. 1959. *A Husband and a Farm in Rhodesia.* Gwelo: Catholic Mission Press.

Boggie, Jeannie M. 1966. *First Steps in Civilizing Rhodesia: Being a True Account of the Experiences of the Earliest White Settlers – Men, Women and Children – in Southern and Northern Rhodesia. Bulawayo: Kingstons.*

Bold, JD. 1990. *Fanagalo: Book, Grammar, Dictionary.* Pretoria: JL van Schaik.

Cary, Robert, and Diana Mitchell. 1977. *African Nationalist Leaders in Rhodesia, Who's Who.* Bulawayo: Books of Rhodesia.

Constitutional Conference, Lancaster House, London, Report of. September-December 1979. 1980. London: HMSO.

Daily Mail, The.

Daily News. Harare, Zimbabwe.

Daily Telegraph, The.

Da Silva, Vicky. 25 February 2002. *The Land Issue in Zimbabwe.* Electoral Institute of Southern Africa.

Economist, The. London.

Edwards, Norna. *Jumbo Guide to Rhodesia 1973–4.* Salisbury, Southern Rhodesia: Wilrey Publications.

Ferris, NS. 1956. *Know Your Rhodesia and Know Nyasaland.* Salisbury: Rhodesian Printing and Publishing Co.

Financial Gazette, The. Harare.

Gale, WD. 1935. *One Man's Vision: The Story of Rhodesia.* London: Hutchinson.

Gelder, Michael, Paul Harrison and Philip Cowen, 2006. *Shorter Oxford Textbook of Psychiatry.* Oxford: Oxford University Press.

Goodall, Elizabeth, CK Cooke and J Desmond Clark. 1959. *Prehistoric Rock Art of the Federation of Rhodesia and Nyasaland*. Salisbury: National Publications Trust.
Guardian, The. London
Gwelo Times, The. Gwelo, Southern Rhodesia.
Hall, Richard. 21 November 1965, 'White Rhodesians: How They Got There.' *The Observer Magazine*, London.
Harris, Julie. *My Memoirs*.
Healey, Denis. 1990. *The Time of My Life*. New York: WW Norton.
Herald, The. Zimbabwe Newspapers Ltd., Herald House, Avenue, Harare, Zimbabwe.
House, Margaret, House, John and Salt, Beryl. 1983. *Zimbabwe: A Handbook*. Harare: Mercury Press.
Independent, The. London
Magadza, Chris. 2006. *Father and other poems*. Poetry International Web 2006.
Meredith, Martin. 2002. *Mugabe: Power and Plunder in Zimbabwe*. Oxford: Public Affairs.
Michie, WD, Kadzombe ED and Naidoo MR. 1983. *Lands and Peoples of Central Africa*. Harlow, Essex, UK: Longman.
Middleton, John (ed.). 1997. *Encyclopaedia of Africa South of the Sahara*. New York: C. Scribner's Sons.
Observer, The.
Ogrizek, Dore. 1954 *South and Central Africa*. New York: McGraw-Hill.
Oliver, Roland and Fage JD. 1988. *A Short History of Africa* (6th ed.). New York: Penguin Books.
Paul, Richard. 1964. *Kaunda: Founder of Zambia*. Zambia: Longmans.
Phillips, Tom, (ed.). 1995. *Africa: The Art Of The Continent*. New York: Prestel.
Rhodesia Herald, The. Salisbury.
Rosenthal, Eric (editor and compiler). 1973. *Encyclopaedia of Southern Africa*. London: Frederick Warne & Co.
Rotberg, Robert I. 1988. *The Founder: Cecil Rhodes and the Pursuit of Power*. Oxford: Oxford University Press.
Royle, Trevor. 1996. Winds of Change: The End of Empire in Africa. London: John Murray.
Salt, Beryl (ed.). 1978. *Extracts from the* Rhodesia Herald. Salisbury, Rhodesia: Galaxie Press.
Smith, David and Simpson C, with Davies, Ian. 1981. *Mugabe*. London: Sphere Books.
Smith, Ian Douglas. 2001. *Bitter Harvest: The Great Betrayal*. London: Blake Publishing.
Southern Rhodesian Constitution, London. June 1961. London: HMSO.
Standard, The. Harare.
Sunday Herald, The. Harare.
Sunday Times, The. London.
Thomas, Antony. 1997. *Rhodes: The Race for Africa*. London: Penguin.
Times, The. London.

Todd, Judith. 2007. *Through the Darkness: A Life in Zimbabwe*. Cape Town: Zebra Press.
Tutu, Desmond. 1999. *No Future without Forgiveness.* London: Rider.
Vindex, Rev. FV. 1900. *Cecil Rhodes: His Political Life and Speeches.* London: Chapman & Hall.
Weekend Tribune, The. Media Africa Group, www.africaonline.com.
Welensky, Sir Roy. 1964. *Welensky's 4,000 Days: The Life and Death of the Federation of Rhodesia and Nyasaland.* London: Collins.
Williams, Basil. 1921. *Cecil Rhodes.* London: Constable.
ZANU-PF website (and presidential website),
20Bio/bio_main.htm

Index